For the Love of Christopher
A Father's Tale
by Ian Paul Lomax
ISBN: 978-0-9926563-3-1

For the Love of Christopher
A Father's Tale
by Ian Paul Lomax

ISBN: 978-0-9926563-3-1

Published by

i2i Publishing. Manchester.
www.i2ipublishing.co.uk

Dedication:

I would like to dedicate this book to my mother who was my rock.

She picked me up when I was down and helped me through the most difficult time of my life. She gave me so much love and hope and a shoulder to cry on. I thank her for always being there for me.

I must also thank:- Jack, my step-dad R.I.P, who stood by me in my battles in the Greek courts; my wife Suzi for her support and my children Amy-Louise and Adam for always showing me love and understanding.

It would be remiss if I did not mention my sister Diane who came to Greece to fight on my behalf; my friend Remanos, the Greek policeman, my other sisters Pat and Denise and my brothers Mark, Stephen and Derek.

A special tribute must also be made to the Bolton Evening News and the people of Bolton who have supported me through all those difficult times.

It is also important to express special thanks to my friends Vera Burrows, Dorothy Martland MBE, her husband Alan Martland and Billy Isherwood for his advice. Without them this book would not have been possible.

As for my son, Christopher, the raison d'etre for this entire book; I thank him for being my son and the love he has given me even though we were separated by land and sea

My final thoughts go to Maria, my ex-Mother-in-Law. Her actions against me, culminating in throwing my suitcase down the stairs and saying I would never see my wife and child again, gave me the strength and resolve to carry on the fight to be a father to my son Christopher.

Ian Paul Lomax

Introduction

If you are looking for a true story that is written from the heart and pulls at your heart-strings, read on.

Whilst writing this book, I have made every effort to tell my side of the story honestly. It has been very difficult for me and very emotional. I want people to understand what I went through and that fathers can bleed and feel pain like any mother can. For the parents who are going through the same pain as I did, I would like them to know there is light at the end of the tunnel. One day your child will come home.

I was born in 1958 in an old mill town called Farnworth, near Bolton in Lancashire. I was one of seven children. I made my entrance into the world in a home that only knew poverty and violence. We children had no choice, but to wear clothes from jumble sales and accept help from the odd charity donation and from family and friends. We were so poor, my dad made me go on building sites and pinch wood because we couldn't afford to buy coal for the fire.

Every Friday night though, we had a treat. My mum used to send me to the fish and chip shop with a big bowl for chips and pea juice, hoping we would get bigger helpings. I felt like Oliver Twist - Please sir, can I have some more?

My brothers and I were a joke around school. Our classmates used to call us the Beatles, because we all had the same hair styles. Looking back, we had haircuts like the old basin cuts – you know, when your mum put a pudding basin on your head and cut around the rim. I used to get into trouble almost every day, but only because I was defending my family honour. If I didn't get a black eye at school, I would get one from my dad for not fighting hard enough.

My father was very strict and a bit of bully and I suffered by his hand on many occasions. I was often sent upstairs to my room as punishment for my bad behaviour, but I used to sneak out through my box-room window to meet up with my friends. When I was fourteen, I ran away from home and went to Paris. I'd had enough of living in fear of my father every day. I stayed there for four days, sleeping in the back of wagons and stealing bread from the local boulangerie to survive. I was eventually picked up by the French police and taken to the British Embassy in Paris. I stayed there all night as a guest. The Embassy officials telephoned my mother and spoke to her. "We have your son," they informed her.

"Why? Where is he?" my bewildered mother asked.

"He's in Paris."

There was silence before I heard my mother exclaim, "Paris? I'll bloody kill him when he gets home!"

Looking back, it seems I was never afraid of striking out on my own to find pastures new. I certainly used that trait in my character after I met the woman of my dreams, but all that will be revealed later.

I left home at the age of sixteen because I'd had enough of my dad's constant bullying. We, especially my mother, had suffered from his bullying actions on many occasions. I detested him for it and felt I needed to protect my mother from him. She was always there for me, my rock and a shoulder to cry on and she proved her love for me throughout my life. Her love and devotion were crucial to my surviving what happened to me and it is all related in these pages.

I drifted through life with several failed relationships. Drastic though it may seem to the average man in the street, I joined the French Foreign Legion to get away from all my troubles. It was a case of out of the frying pan into the fire for me as I received a beating almost every day for six weeks and it was a complete nightmare. This is where I learned the truth in the saying, necessity is the mother of invention and bending the truth was sometimes the only way to keep control of your own life. I pretended that I was going to self-harm and the only way I could get out was with a dishonourable discharge. I didn't care. I had regained my dignity away from a regime that was completely alien to me.

I tried to settle down with various women, but I couldn't live with them. They all wanted different things from me, but I was just looking to be loved. When I did fall in love ...well, that is really where my story begins.

Out of the blue, I received a call from my mother to tell me my father was seriously ill in hospital. "I don't care," I told her. "He doesn't deserve any affection from me after the way he treated me." It was callous, but nonetheless meant.

"Please, Ian," my mother pleaded. "Go to see him. If not for him, do it for me. Make peace with him before he dies."

When I arrived at the hospital my mother was already there. My father was in a side ward, wired up to all kinds of monitors. I sat next to him and actually felt sorry for him for the first time in years. He held out his hand and I held it. He looked at me and he was mumbling something I couldn't understand. Now, I hope he said sorry, but I'll never know. He held my hand so tightly and then peacefully slipped away. I suddenly felt the pain I thought I would never experience. I felt a sudden sense of loss and I was really glad that I had made my peace with him before he died. I felt so much remorse and grief, I was confused. Deep down, I must have loved him. I just wish he had told me he loved me. I said my final goodbyes to him, determined I would turn my life around, turn my back on my past troubles and start a new chapter in my life. I knew that if I ever had a son, I would love him with all my heart and soul and do everything in my power to show him that love.

I decided I needed a holiday and a change of scenery and so my story begins...

For the Love of Christopher

Chapter 1 - Love will find a way.

It was a momentary decision. The thought came into my head to take a holiday in Greece. I'd always fancied going. It would be nice to get away to see the sights and also I thought it would be a bit of an adventure. Had I known this decision to take a short break, would turn into the longest and worst ordeal I was ever going to face; I might have decided differently. As it turned out, it took me down roads I certainly didn't want to go. The only driving force that saw me through the hardest times was the love for my son and love can indeed move mountains. I later realised that was exactly what faced me.

Everybody has a tale to tell. I have met people whose lives have been remarkable and inspiring. I hope my story will be just as inspiring and illuminating for those who find themselves in a similar position to me.

In 1990 whilst on the holiday in Corfu I met a Greek girl named Helen. Little did I know that this first encounter was to change both our lives forever? I had fallen head over heels in love with her and likewise, she with me.

I only knew Helen for three days and three nights, not long really, but nevertheless ever minute I spent with her was incredibly worthwhile.

The first time I ever saw Helen was when I was sitting in the bar of my hotel in Benitses. It was only 3pm in the afternoon. It was a small bar but well stocked up with the cocktails I liked.

The cocktail I drank was called Blue Wave and was a mixture of gin, white rum, blue Curacao, pineapple juice, lime juice and finished off with a couple of dashes of syrup and crushed ice .

(I suffered from the effects of that drink with severe bouts of headaches during the whole time I was on holiday there.)

Three young girls walked into the bar. I could hear them speaking Greek and I thought to myself that they were good looking girls.

One of them caught my attention straight away. She stood out from the two other girls. She had long beautiful blonde hair which hung half way down her back and she was wearing a blue swimsuit with beach sandals.

The other two girls were quite pretty. They were also wearing blue swimsuits and just plain sandals

Two of the girls went straight into the hotel and the girl I liked sat next to me at the bar and smiled at me a few times with her beautiful blue eyes.

I thought to myself wow she's so beautiful. I could feel butterflies in my stomach. I'm not a shy guy usually as I have had my fair share of women but Helen was something different.

She had a sexy Greek accent which turned me on straight away. I built up my courage and said hello. She replied back in broken English and said, "Hi, how are you?"

I replied nervously that my name was Ian and she then told me that her name was Helen.

I put out my hand to her and she shook my hand which was trembling.

She was drinking a soft drink; just ordinary orange juice, I think.

I was thinking to myself, all the time I was looking at her, that she was very beautiful and that it would be a dream come true, if she liked me.

I could not stop looking at her. To me she looked like a Greek goddess. I was oblivious to what was going on around me.

She didn't stay long in the bar with me; she wanted to go back for a shower and to have a sleep.

She got up and smiled and was ready to walk away. I just grabbed her and told her, speaking slowly in my Farnworth accent, that I wanted to see her again.

She shrugged her shoulders and looked at me and said in her broken English, "Eight pm here in the bar."

I understood what she was trying to say. God knows how she understood my Farnworth dialect as most people, even in England, struggled to understand me.

Anyway she left and said goodbye in her sexy accent. I carried on and downed a few more drinks, just to calm my nerves. I didn't drink anything strong; I just had a couple of small Ouzos. I didn't stay long after Helen went, probably no more than half an hour.

While I was drinking I was just thinking of Helen, how charming and polite she was.

I left the bar and went straight back to my hotel room where I had a quick shower. I put on my best white short-sleeved shirt, jeans and black shoes. I made sure I smelled nice by spraying under my arms and I put on Kouros, my favourite aftershave. It was one of the best available at the time.

I peered at myself in the mirror so many times that I knew exactly how many spots I had on my face.

I arrived at the hotel bar early. It was only six thirty and I wasn't supposed to be meeting her till 8pm

I drank a few vodkas for Dutch courage. I don't know why I felt so nervous. The bar was about half-full. There were probably no more than thirty people sitting there.

Ian and Helen - 1990

Now time was getting on; it was nearly 9pm and I was getting worried she wasn't going to turn up.

My heart sank, I was feeling a bit upset. I can't explain the reason but I knew she was something special. And then I saw her walking into the bar. I will never forget the moment. Her hair was so blond and so straight and it was half-way down her back.

She was wearing a white blouse which was quite low and I could see that she had ample breasts. She was also wearing black pants with black shoes. I looked at her face. Her blue eyes were sparkling and with her bright red luscious lips she looked a real picture.

My heart was pounding when she said hello. I just couldn't get any words to come out of my mouth. All I could do was to look into her eyes.

When I came out of my trance I was just mesmerised by her beauty. I asked her what she was drinking she replied that it was just an ouzo.

Conversation was difficult. We could hardy understand each other. The only way to get over this was to sometimes write things down on pieces paper, to make it easier to comprehend. Helen's English was quite poor. She spoke in broken English but it was enough to have a simple conversation.

We wrote down what our names were and how old we were. It was a strange way to converse but I found it entertaining nevertheless.

The night was passing too quickly for my liking so I asked her would she like to walk along on the beach.

She started to shrug her shoulders again, as though she couldn't understand me. So I built up my courage by grabbing her hands which were lovely and soft.

She just followed me, holding my hand. We walked slowly to the beach which was only a few minutes away.

We didn't speak much and we just kept smiling at each other. We soon arrived on the beach and we sat down on a rock. It was then that I put my arms around her and she just put her head on my shoulder as we listened to the waves

I was so comfortable with her it was unreal. It wasn't long before we kissed. Her lips were tender and luscious and we just kissed for what seemed like an hour.

It was so romantic. She stroked my hair while we just looked into each other's eyes

I knew then that I was in falling in love with her. It was such a strange feeling that I had.

I felt that I could have just melted in her arms.

We walked back to the hotel where we were both staying. I really wanted to walk her to her room but I didn't as I didn't want to spoil anything between us and to give her the wrong impression about me.

I said good night to her and I asked her could we meet up tomorrow. She wrote on a scrap of paper, *8pm hotel,* so I just nodded my head and smiled; we kissed a little and off she went.

I had wanted to meet Helen earlier in the day. However, she was on a college trip but I was happy anyway that she wanted to see me again.

I didn't sleep much that first night. I couldn't get Helen out of my head. I loved her and I had from the moment I had met her.

During the day I just went on the beach, had a swim and then sunbathed. I was just passing the time away until I met Helen again.

It was now getting nearer to the time so I went back to hotel and had a shower. I made sure I was dressed ok and smelled nice; all the normal things you do before you go on a date.

Helen was on time. I grabbed her hand and kissed her and then we went for a meal. I ordered all the trimmings, chicken and salad, fish and wine.

Helen was getting quite chatty. I didn't feel nervous any more as I felt so comfortable with her. A young girl came to our table selling roses. I gave her five drachmas. I didn't know the correct price and I didn't care.

I gave the rose to Helen and she bent over and kissed me. Little did I know at the time that the red rose I gave her was a symbol of our love?

We were laughing as she taught me a few Greek words and I was teaching her English words.

Then I just came out and told her that I loved her very much. I didn't get the chance to feel embarrassed and she replied and said, "I love you Ian."

That night went pretty well and we walked along the beach again holding hands. After a while we headed back, stopping and kissing frequently on the way.

We soon reached the hotel and we kissed and hugged to wish each other good-night. Then she told me again that she loved me. It was a good ending to what was a very special night.

The following day was her last day as she was going back to Athens along with her college friends. After all, it was her college trip. She decided, however, to spend the last day with me until she left which would be at nine pm.

I met her early which was at ten am. I had already booked a coach to Kavos which wasn't that far from our resort, Benitses.

Kavos was on the southern tip of the island and was very popular in the 80s and was the night-life capital of the island.

She arrived on time and off we went on the trip. It took us an hour or so to get there. When we arrived we just walked around the resort, along the large sandy beach. From there we could see all the water-sports activities that were going on; jet skiing and water skiing. We had a few drinks along the way in the beach bars which were mainly small cocktail bars with English music in the background.

We went for a meal and I made it as special as I could for her. We had a fish Plata with sword fish and a variety of other kinds of fish, followed by the best Greek wine.

We held each other's hands and smiled a lot. We kissed repeatedly and told each other how much we loved each other.

We then went to Corfu town on one of the local busses which only took an hour.

Corfu town is Venice and Naples, a touch of France and more than a dash of England. It has a maze of narrow streets dominated by the 16 century fortress. Around every corner you can find a Chapel, an old mansion or a secret garden square.

Helen wanted to go round the shops and buy some souvenirs to take home with her. She bought me a friendship ring. I did the same. It was only cheap but it was a symbol of love between us.

We then went to a small cafe which was up a side street; you could smell the coffee aroma and the local pastries.

We spent a few more hours in Corfu town. It was a pleasant experience. We had seen some beautiful Venetian architecture and tasted the local delicacies and visited some of the local shops.

Sadly it was 'go back' day and it had passed very quickly. On the return drive to the hotel she put her head on my shoulders.

I started to feel really sad that her holiday was coming to an end. She called me her English prince. She knew where I was from and about my family; even what football team I supported.

And I knew a little about where she was from and about her family. We had talked about all this on the second night.

The coach had arrived back in Benitses and it was now ten pm and her coach was leaving at eleven. We walked back to the hotel and we kissed and we arranged to meet at 10.45 outside the hotel where her coach was picking her up, along with her college friends. They had been there on a college project about the history of Corfu.

I didn't go back into my room. I went into the hotel bar and had a few cocktails. It was now quarter to eleven and Helen was there. She grabbed my hand and hugged me and told me she loved me. We kissed and then she said that she had to go. My heart sank as I looked into her beautiful blue eyes.

She started to cry and this set me off. A few tears rolled down the sides of my cheeks. She let go of my hand and said to me, "I will love you always," and she jumped onto the coach

She sat down by a window where she could see me. I saw tears rolling down her cheeks. I was sad. I felt so lost without her. The coach started to pull out; she blew a kiss to me and she was gone.

The coach was now out of sight. I sat down on a bench. I felt so empty inside. I had tears rolling down the sides of my face. I just put my head in my hands and I cried profusely. I felt so much pain in a way I had never felt before.

After Helen had gone home, for the last two days of my trip I just wandered around, lost like in some hypnotic trance. My heart ached for her and everywhere I went was just a haunting memory of the places we had been so happy together. I just couldn't get her out of my heart and head and I didn't want to either.

I never thought I would see her again and tried to convince myself that it was just a holiday romance but I knew deep down that this was something special. Little did I know, three weeks after my return home, back in England, I would receive a letter with an invitation to visit her in Athens? My heart was beating so fast and my hands were shaking as I read and re-read that letter. If only I had known then how that letter was to impact on my life and turn it upside down. If only I had known then that the holiday dream romance I'd spent with Helen would turn into a nightmare.

The flight back to England had been a quiet one. I was deep in thought and couldn't get Helen out of my mind. I had left my heart in Corfu with the girl of my dreams. I had already decided, before I landed back in England that I would be going back to Greece to be with Helen and then the letter had arrived.

Ian arriving in Greece

I arrived in Athens bright and early as it was a night flight and very pleasant. I had meal on the journey. It wasn't anything special; chicken, a few peas and vegetables followed by a drink of orange juice. All through the flight I had butterflies. I just couldn't wait for the plane to land. Finally, I arrived in Athens about 3am in the morning.

The airport wasn't very modern. It was small and just looked like a large run-down building but it was packed with bustling holiday-makers. I collected my suit case and exited the airport.

Outside the airport there were plenty of yellow taxis. I walked straight past them as I had no intentions of catching any of them. I had heard that they was infamous for ripping people off.

I caught a bus to Piraeus which was an experience in itself. It was packed to the rafters. You couldn't even move your elbows as everybody was crammed in like sardines. I was lucky to get a seat. The trip to Piraeus took over one hour and along the way I had never seen so many people on mopeds. None of them had helmets on and some even had children on the back. It seemed road safety wasn't an issue there. I arrived in Piraeus around 5.30 am and alighted near the metro station which was the link to all the districts in Athens.

Piraeus was a bustling port and it is where all the cruise liners sailed from to the Greek islands.

I was feeling very hungry so I went to a small cafe in the little square facing the metro station. I sat down and had a coffee and some toast and I watched the comings and goings in the square. It was fascinating. There were interesting people of many different nationalities milling around and mixed in with them were people who were begging.

I found it incredible that there were so many foreigners and beggars in one place as I had never seen that before.

The beggars would come into the cafe and give their sob stories and ask for money. They had small cards in their hands and they would put them on the tables hoping that diners would pick them up and read them.

I briefly read one and it stated that the man had cancer. He had no job and he had to feed his family and so on. And I had to admit he looked the part as he was dressed in old clothes which smelt like he had never had a wash for years. I felt sorry for him so I gave him a few drachmas and off he went to the next table.

All the time that I spent in Athens this would be a common practice. There were literally thousands of beggars; some were genuine and some were not.

It was now 9 am and it was time; time to make my way to Helens house in Perama which was a district in Piraeus.

Helen had sent me instructions as to what bus to catch. It was a green bus number 543. I had no problem finding the stop as it was right outside the metro station.

It was only 9am in the morning and already very hot, somewhere in the mid 70s. This was a summer temperature in England. I was glad I was just wearing my Bolton Wanderers top, shorts and trainers as I was already sweating in the morning heat.

I set of on my short journey to Helen's house. I was so excited that I had butterflies running riot through my stomach. It was an interesting journey I looked at all the landscapes and what kind of houses the people lived in. Most of the homes were painted white and immaculate.

On the left side of the road you could see the beautiful blue sea and a small island in the distance which was called Salamis. It was here that the Greek fleet destroyed the Persian fleet in the Greek and Persian wars all those years ago.

Eventually I arrived at my bus stop. Reality was now sinking in. *I was here in Helen's neighbourhood.*

My heart was missing a beat and my legs felt like jelly. It was only three weeks since I had met Helen but I felt it was like a lifetime ago.

I walked slowly up the steep hill which seemed to last forever.

Her house was at the top of this long winding road. I was totally exhausted. The road seemed to last forever. It was like walking up a mountain as it was so steep. Even the taxis seemed to struggle as they chugged along trying to get any kind of speed up.

As I climbed I was listening to my music tape. It was Two Hearts by Phil Collins. They used to play this song repeatedly in the hotel bar in Corfu where Helen and I had met up. It was the song we picked to remind us how much we loved each other.

I nearly reached the top of the hill but I had to sit down as I was totally worn out. I looked at all the houses and wondered what kind of people lived in them.

How were they dressed? I was curious about the Greek culture. I had heard so much about.

People who were walking past me were fascinated by the way I was dressed and looked at my tattoos. I could see them judging me and thinking I was some kind of football hooligan. That is how they saw all English men with tattoos. They had seen all the football violence splashed all over the news on their television sets.

Then I could see Helen waving to me as she waited for me on the balcony. I approached her house which was pure white and built like a maisonette.

I walked up the steps and there was Helen. She looked exactly the same as she was in Corfu when I had first met her.

I smiled at her and she hugged me and said, "Hi my English prince," which was what she called me in Corfu and right up until we separated in 1998.

We went inside the house. There were Greek vases everywhere, and the floor had marble tiles.

The marble tiles were beautifully veined and polished to a high gloss which enhanced natural light and space.

The house was immaculate. Pictures were all over the walls and there were even Greek statues in the corners of the room. And then there was a small bar with every drink you could think off.

I saw this women come towards me. I guessed it must be Helen's mother. She was wearing a pink nightgown. She was quite tubby with short bleached hair. She shook my hand and said, "Hello Ian," in her broken English accent.

She certainly had a presence about her. As I would find out later, she seemed to dominate Helen. She was barking out orders to her that I didn't understand, as I didn't speak any Greek, but it was her straight face and loud voice which perturbed me.

I didn't see her stepdad who was called Vangelis until later in the evening. He was a taxi driver and worked long hard shifts.

Helen showed me where I was sleeping. I thought I was getting my own room but she pointed to a leather sofa in the living room. I thought that was fine until she told me her mother's bedroom was facing me. Little did I know at the time that this was an excuse for Maria to keep an eye on me.

I was so happy to be with her again that I would give Helen a kiss at every opportunity when her mum turned her back on us. We were like two school kids even though I was 32 and Helen was only 20 at the time.

Maria had made lunch which was equivalent to our High Tea in England. While we sat at the dining table the door opened and in came Vangelis, Maria's husband. He was quite tall and of medium build with jet black hair. He was clean-shaven.

Vangelis was a couple of years younger than me but looked a lot older as his face was quite wrinkled either from the hot sun or from pressure of work.

He looked like a typical Greek, very serious and proud. He shook my hand and then we all sat down at the table together.

Helen was all smiles with me. I could see Maria and Vangelis observing me by looking me up and down and looking at my tattoos which they both seemed fascinated with. I didn't know at the time but most of the Greeks never saw people with tattoos unless they worked on the ships. They classed people with tattoos as criminals who went to prison and I found this quite troubling. Wherever I went in Athens the Greeks used to stare at me all the time.

The food was typical Greek food. For example there was chicken and salad, with chips and various other kinds of Greek cuisine. It took me a while to get used to all the olive oil and the garlic in the food but I adjusted to it even though it didn't do my stomach any good.

The first couple of days she showed me round the village where she lived. It was just a typical village with mostly white houses. They had beautiful red flowers and all the houses had balconies with table and chairs.

There was few cafe bars with Greek music in the back ground and which served a small variety of drinks. They also served simple foods like pizza and Souvlaki.

Helen introduced me to a couple of her friends. One was called Malpo who was as mad as a hatter. She was about twenty five stone but she was a lovely girl who I got on very well with. Helen had a very close friendship with Malpo but warned me she was very loud and loved to lark about in front of people and didn't care who was watching. But she told me she was funny and fun to be with although absolutely crazy.

The other was a Scottish girl who was married to a Greek guy who was called Stavros. He was actually some relation to Helen's mother.

Valerie was a girl I really got on very well with and in time we would become very good friends. She was another close friend of Helen's. She told me Valerie was very loyal and always there if she needed her; if she ever had problems with anything. Valerie already knew about me as Helen had told her about how we met in Corfu. We visited her a few times at her house which was quite simple but very nice just the same. It was beautifully decorated with cream walls and covered in lovely pictures of Greek white houses on mountains, with beautiful coloured flowers surrounded by the deep blue sea. She had Greek statues in the hallway and lovely red flowers in large plant pots. Her floor had lovely plain white tiles with different small coloured flowers on them.

It was Valerie who forewarned me about Helen's mother; what she was like which I would find out for myself as the holiday progressed. Valerie also told me that Maria, Helen's mother was very strict with her upbringing. Helen wasn't allowed to have any boyfriends. She did off course, which she had to keep secret.

Valerie also told me that Maria had brought her up like a little girl even though she was twenty years old and if she ever went out anywhere she had to ring her mother and tell where she was.

Valerie was painting a bad picture of Maria for me. I was getting a bit worried about what I was letting myself in for.

After a few days, however, I put all that to the back of mind as Vangelis and Maria were being quite nice with me.

One morning I was delighted when Maria told Helen to inform me that if I wanted to stay for a few weeks longer I could, as they were enjoying my company.

I was very pleased as it enabled me to spend a lot more time with Helen and now I would be able to see all the sites in Athens like Plaka and the Acropolis.

We got up one early one morning as promised and Helen took me to Plaka which is the historical neighbourhood of Athens. It is clustered around the northern and eastern slopes of the Acropolis and incorporates labyrinthine streets and neoclassical architecture.

We spent a few hours there. It was a magical place and was easy to get to on the underground metro with all its links to the districts of Athens.

Then we went to the Acropolis, one of the seven wonders of the ancient world, a place I used to dream about in my younger days.

The Acropolis of Athens is an ancient citadel located on a high rocky outcrop above the city of Athens and containing the remains of several ancient buildings of great architectural and historic significance. The most famous is the Parthenon.

Athens is the capital and largest city of Greece. Athens dominates the Attica region and is one of the world's oldest cities, with its recorded history spanning around 3,400 years. It is a city with the most glorious history in the world, a city worshipped by gods and people, a magical city. It is known as the birthplace of civilisation. It was the city where democracy was born and was populated by the wisest men of ancient times. It had one of the most important civilisations of the ancient world.

The Acropolis of Athens and its monuments are universal symbols of the classical spirit and civilisation and form the greatest architectural and artistic complex bequeathed by Greek Antiquity to the world.

Ian at the Acropolis

I was just mesmerised at the beautiful marble arches of the Parthenon and I took many photographs to remind me of this magical day.

I was walking around in a trance. I couldn't believe what I was seeing; it was a truly amazing place and full of history.

We wandered around the Plaka looking for a nice Taverna and were studying the menu outside one such establishment, when we were grabbed by the owner's son. He persuaded us to take a chance on his food...Boy did it pay off.

Being tired we let our waiter make decisions for us... Fried cheese and a Greek salad for starters... The Feta cheese was fantastic... Whole snapper for our main course... Our waiter filleted the fish at our table... It was cooked perfectly... Fresh fruit to finish with a cold ouzo...

We had had a fantastic day in a magical place and finished it off with a romantic meal.

It was now 10pm and it was getting quite dark so we headed off to a Taverna in Piraeus.

Helen knew the bar very well as she visited there with her friends. It was called the Alexandra bar. It was only small but very traditional and colourful with bottles all along the wall. It was a very friendly place with a very friendly atmosphere.

In the background they played typical Greek music and on the odd occasion when Helen and I visited the bar a waiter would play the violin which gave an added flavour of romance.

The days were flying by now and I was already in the third week. Helen's mother suggested that we should visit her grandparents on Ikaria.

Icaria also spelled Ikaria is a Greek Island in the Aegean Sea, ten nautical miles southwest of Samos. It derived its name from Icarus the son of Daedalus in Greek mythology.

We both agreed as it was an excuse to get away from her mother Maria's suspicious and watchful eyes and spend some time on our own.

We sailed in the morning in what turned out to be an uneventful trip although we were both seasick. In fact we never ventured outside our cabin and we slept most of the trip which took over nine hours.

We arrived safely and were met by her grandfather. He was only small, in his sixties and softly spoken.

He took us to his house in the back of a small trailer towed by a small tractor.

The journey took us along winding roads and up a mountain. It was very scenic and we saw the odd goat and even a few rabbits. It was over forty five minutes before we reached the house.

Waiting for us was Helen's grandma. She was a typical Greek woman, small and wearing a red head scarf.

We entered the house it was very old and looked like a run-down shack with wooden windows and concrete floors.

She showed us the room we were both staying in and to my surprise she said to Helen, "You make up your own mind, who sleeps on the couch and who sleeps on the bed?"

This brought a massive smile to my face as I knew I would have the opportunity to make love to Helen and not under the watchful eyes of her mother, Maria.

The bedroom was full of cobwebs and the windows were old and broken. But I didn't care.

Helen took me outside and showed me around the grounds. Her granddad had an orchard filled with apples, oranges and lemons.

He even grew his own grapes and the house was surrounded by olive trees where he made his own olive oil.

I looked out over the mountain to where I could see the beautiful beaches and the deep blue sea,

It was a beautiful island. We had a few odd cuddles out of the view of her grandparents and I was longing for the night time when I would make love to her for the very first time.

In Corfu I never had a chance so I did not want to give this opportunity up.

It was now time for our evening meal. We had chips and soup and goat. It was the first time I had ever tasted it. It tasted like chicken but was quite tough.

Fruit was plentiful so was the wine which her granddad made himself.

I pretended to her grandma that I was tired but really I just wanted Helen in bed and I couldn't wait any longer.

I left the table and waited for Helen. It was only a matter of minutes before she followed me.

We locked the door and we started kissing gently but then they turned into passionate kisses. I undressed her slowly and then we made passionate love throughout the night. It was wonderfully sensuous and very romantic. Afterwards she slept in my arms all night. We repeated the experience every night of our stay.

Each day we went to the beach a few times and swam in the sea which was calm and quite warm.

The week passed so quickly and it wasn't long before we were sailing back to Piraeus.

It was a great trip and a lovely experience living on a mountain.

I was to go home in a week so I had wanted to make it a week that we would both remember.

I asked Helen would she like to come to England with me and she agreed.

When we arrived at the house Maria was in different mood. Maria had found out from her mother, Helen's grandma that we had slept in the same room. She was screaming at Helen I was getting worried but the shouting stopped fairly quickly. However, Maria's attitude towards me changed and for the rest of the time I was there, it went from bad to worse.

We kept out of her way whenever we could. One day, on a day out in Piraeus with Helen we were kissing like young couples do outside the metro station. Little did we know that one of Vangelis' friends, who was a taxi driver, saw us and telephoned Maria.

When we arrived at Helen's house, Maria was waiting for us on the balcony. As soon as we arrived she slapped Helen.

I was shocked. She was screaming at the top of her voice that someone saw her kissing me and that we had shamed her.

I didn't know what to do so I just stayed on the stairs.

It was then that Helen asked Maria permission for her to go to England with me. That made the shouting even louder.

Helen came storming out and she was crying. I grabbed her and took away from the house.

She was shaking and crying. I felt so sorry for her.

We went in to Piraeus and I booked a hotel for the night. I managed to calm her down and asked her what all the shouting was about. She explained that her mother had refused to let her go to England.

I said to her, "She can't stop you as you are an adult." She then replied in her broken voice and said this is Greece and not England. It was something I was to discover in the not too distant future.

We made passionate love again all night. I didn't care too much about Maria. I was with Helen and that's all that mattered to me.

In the morning we both returned to Helen's house. This time Maria and Vangelis were waiting for us. They told us to sit down. It was Vangelis who then told Helen to tell me that I must go back to England as soon as I could get a flight home.

Maria told Helen in a soft voice to tell me that her life was in Greece with her mother.

I didn't say a word. I was very quiet and numb.

I looked at Helen she was was very quiet and didn't answer back in a bad way to her mother and Vangelis. She felt that she had to accept the situation.

My holiday romance was coming to an end. I now realised it was time to go home back to England and I was leaving anyway the following day.

On the last night we didn't go out. We stayed in and sat on the balcony all night drinking wine and ouzo. I was determined to make it as pleasant as possible for her. I told Helen many times that night that I would always love her and she would be in my heart for ever. I held her and she cried in my arms.

I loved her so much and now it was coming to an end. I was desperately sorry for her as she was living in an environment where her mother was intolerably strict with her and she had no freedom.

Maria was house crazy. She was obsessed with cleaning all the time. You couldn't drop a crumb on the floor without her sweeping it up straight away. She even wiped the creases off the couch when you got up and worst of all, as soon as she knew you were out of bed she would wipe all the creases out of the sheets.

I was leaving poor Helen behind to all this craziness and sadness. She had no life in Greece. She was a prisoner in all but name.

The morning had arrived; it was time to leave. My suitcase was packed and I was ready to go.

I said my goodbyes to Maria and Vangelis who shook my hand and wished me a good trip. I looked at Helen with my sad eyes and said, "Are you coming to the airport?"

Helen looked at her mother and at Vangelis waiting for an answer and it was then to his credit that Vangelis said he would take us both to the airport.

I originally booked the flight to Athens for one week but I had stayed for five weeks in total. I wasn't working at the time. I was actually unemployed so time wasn't of the essence.

We left for the airport. It didn't take long; about forty five minutes in total.

I held Helen in my arms on the back seat. I could see Vangelis watching through his mirror. I just didn't care what Vangelis thought, every minute was precious to me. I was leaving behind the girl I truly loved and I didn't want the visit to end.

We arrived at the airport and Vangelis got out and opened the car boot to get my suitcase out. Helen got out and said goodbye to me and kissed me and held me for a few moments.

Then that was it and Vangelis told Helen to get back in the car and they drove away.

I was so numb, I felt empty. It was time to check in and fly back home with a broken heart. I promised myself that I would never forget my Corfu girl.

When I had arrived in Athens, I was supposed to be visiting for just one week, but I stayed for five. Those five weeks were the best times of my life. Helen and I grew very close while we were together and during the last week when I was preparing to go home, she told her mother she wanted to go to England so we could be together. Helen was nineteen years old and her mother had refused point blank to give her permission to travel to England with me. I was under no illusions whatsoever when her mother, Maria said to me, "You go back to England. Helen stays here."

I left the girl I loved with a broken heart. She was forced to stay in Greece under the watchful eye of her mother. She was almost a prisoner in her own home. Maria still treated Helen as a little child. She wasn't allowed to wear make-up or to have boyfriends. I interpreted that as meaning she wasn't free to love and have feelings.

I arrived in England alone on that fateful Friday morning and as crazy as it may seem, the following day, driven by love, I made a hasty decision to hitch-hike back to Greece. Within a couple of hours, I had packed and was ready to leave. I had no plans and very little money. I checked on how much cash I had. It wasn't much - one hundred and eighty pounds in total. I just wanted to be with Helen and that's all I cared about. I didn't sleep much that night. I was thinking about how I was going to get to Athens with so little money, but come hell or high water, I was determined to do it.

All I knew was that I was going to go by coach to London and then another coach to Dover. I would have to find my way across France and Italy before taking a boat across the Adriatic Sea to Greece. I didn't have the money for a flight so by land and sea was my only option. The journey to London was long, but uneventful and after a further two hour trip, I landed in Dover where I booked a single ticket on the ferry to Calais. I had taken enough food to last me for a few days. I didn't know how long I was staying in Greece, or if I ever wanted to go back to England.

As luck would have it, I met a family from Bristol on the ferry. They were Julie, James and their children, Edward and Mark. They had a campervan and were aiming to travel through France to Milan, Italy. It was inevitable that they would ask where I was going and they were shocked to hear that I would even attempt to hitch-hike to Greece. When I told them about Helen, however, they understood my need. I simply wanted to be with her. I missed her so much and my life was empty without her.

"You must be crazy trying to hitch-hike all the way to Greece," they told me, "but if you like, you can come with us until we arrive in Italy. We aren't going as far as you need to go, but it will help you on your way."

"Are you kidding?" I asked in astonishment. "Thank you so much. I can't tell you how grateful I am."

It was a long trip, but very enjoyable. I was more than grateful for the food and a place to rest my head at night. I was in good company and we had interesting conversations. I saw some fascinating places, but I was getting fed up, because all I wanted to do was get to Greece and see my beloved Helen. However, it gave me a chance to stop worrying about Helen for a while and stop wondering what might be waiting for me when I arrived at her door. We arrived in Milan after driving through some memorable places – Reims, Dijon and Mont Blanc. After buying me a meal, the family drove me to the train station and paid for my ticket to Ancona where I could catch the boat to Greece. Julie had packed up some food and water for me to have on my travels. She and James were my guardian angels, that's for sure and I shall never be able to thank them enough.

It wasn't difficult to find the port in Ancona and soon I was on my way to Patras in Greece from where I would easily be able to travel to Athens. The voyage took twenty-three hours. In order to save money, I didn't book a cabin so I slept on the deck when it was possible to find a suitable space. The packed lunch that Julie had given me kept the hunger away so I didn't need to go to the restaurant. I sat on the top deck and watched the ocean as we sailed across the Adriatic Sea to my love.

From Patras, I set off on the relatively short trip to Athens. With every mile I travelled, I was becoming more and more nervous. I didn't know what kind of reception I would receive from Maria and her husband, Vangelis, but I knew Helen would be happy to see me. I needed to spend some time with her and confirm that we had a future together. Personally, I had already made up my mind that I wanted to spend the rest of my life with her, but common sense (I did have some even though my recent rash actions might not suggest that) told me we had to be together for a while. At that point, I didn't care if it were in England or in Greece. I had convinced myself it was more than a holiday romance and I wanted to prove that to Helen's mother, Maria and step-father, Vangelis. I wanted to show them how much I loved Helen. If I had to live in Greece, so be it. I knew I would have to find a job and a place to live to support Helen and make her happy. My intentions were extremely honourable.

I took the green bus to Perama where Helen lived and was dropped off at the bottom of the hill near her house. I sat down on a bench and took a deep breath. The Athens August sun beat down on me, but I needed to collect my thoughts before I approached the house. I hadn't told Helen I was going. I wanted to surprise her. I just hoped she wouldn't be too shocked.

Every nerve in my body was jangling, but my time had come to face Maria and Vangelis, so I started to walk slowly up the hill towards their house. I was afraid; I admit it. I knew Maria and what she was like, but if my love for Helen meant anything at all, I had to prepare myself for what might happen. Helen was sitting on the balcony along with Maria. I saw them before I reached the front door at the top of the steps. Helen was shocked, but happy to see me, but her mother wasn't happy at all.

Maria stood at the top of the steps and harshly shouted down to me, "Go back to England! We don't want you here."

Helen came out to me and said quietly, "Wait for me at the cafe at the bottom of the road."

I waited in the cafe for over an hour and I was on my third bottle of beer, when Helen came rushing down the hill as if she were being chased by a pack of hounds. She had had to sneak out to meet me. She was crying and I put my arms around her to comfort her. She felt so good in my arms and I melted at her touch, the feel of her body next to mine and the delicious scent of her. "I love you," I whispered. "I love you with all my heart and soul."

Gradually she calmed down, but she had to impart bad news. "You can't stay at the house. You are not welcome. My mother says our relationship is finished."

I looked into her eyes. "Do you still want me?" I asked earnestly.

"Yes, I do," she replied.

With that I took her into Piraeus, away from the clutches of her mother. We headed for the Alexandra bar where we used to go when I first went to Athens. We talked for hours, oblivious of what was going on around us. I told Helen straight. "You must come to England with me. You can't stay here, not now. I want you to be free and live a normal life in England with me." We agreed that she would tell her mother she was going back to England with me the following morning. There were to be no arguments. It's what we both wanted.

We stayed out all night and slept on a park bench near her grandma's house. It wasn't cold; in fact it was quite warm even though the temperature of the night air was cooler than it had been during the day. I held Helen in my arms all night and just stared at her. I was stroking her hair and looking forward to our being together not realising the full implications of the situation. When Helen awoke, she said she would go to her grandma's for some food and a drink. I was so tired and I slept on the bench while I was waiting for Helen to return.

Suddenly, I was awakened by her granddad who slapped me across the face. He was shouting at me in Greek. I didn't understand what he was saying, but I knew he was very angry with me.

I jumped up and it was then I saw Maria and Vangelis rushing towards me with three other men I had never seen before. My heart was pounding in my chest. I was truly afraid of what was going to happen to me. Maria started to shove me and told me again to go back to England. Then she kicked my suitcase over and slapped me. Helen sprang to my defence and started fighting with Maria.

The situation was manic. Vangelis attacked me, throwing punches at me from all directions. I had to fight back and I punched him a few times. The coward was lying on the ground screaming like a baby. The three Greek guys jumped on me like a pack of wolves. I couldn't escape. I was being punched and kicked all over the floor. My tee shirt was torn apart and my jeans were ripped. I was covered in blood. Helen was screaming and crying and shouting and then as suddenly as it had started, it stopped. Helen was pushed into a yellow taxi which belonged to Vangelis. I was forced into another taxi with the three Greek guys who had beaten me and I was taken to the police station.

When I arrived, Maria, Vangelis and Helen were already there. I was thrown out of the car along with my suitcase. Vangelis went into the police station. Within minutes a police officer came out and told me that Helen didn't want to go with me. "You must go home," he said.

I looked at Helen. She was in tears and was being held back by Maria and Vangelis. The officer then warned me, "If you don't go home, the family will kill you and I will turn a blind eye to it. We could find you dead on some piece of derelict land."

I had been in many scrapes in the past with gang fights in Farnworth and football punch-ups on a Saturday afternoon following Bolton Wanderers in my younger, more reckless days, but this was on a different scale. I had to go back to England, otherwise there was a distinct possibility I might be found dead on some derelict land like the officer had said and never be seen alive again.

I checked my pockets to make sure I had my passport and my wallet, but my wallet had gone. I must have lost it when I was fighting in the park. I shouted to Vangelis, "I have no money, but I do have my passport. Vangelis smirked as he gave me fifty drachmas saying, "You must go back the way you came." Helen translated to me and Vangelis said, "You will be taken by car to Athens and put on a coach to Patras where you will go by boat to Italy and find your own way home."

Maria stepped forward and spoke to Helen in Greek. Helen translated again. "My mother says you can write to me. Don't worry, I'll be fine."

I gave Helen a hug. She kissed me goodbye then she was taken away. My heart sank and I was put into a taxi with the three Greek guys who were Vangelis' friends. When we arrived at the coach station, I was given my suitcase and they stayed to make sure I left on the coach. It was like a film with a bad ending. I was on the coach alone going back to Patras having to face the long, sad journey home without the girl I loved. It had taken me nearly five days to get there and I had stayed in Greece for just a day and a night.

I arrived in Patras and the first thing I did was to clean up. My face was a mess. I had black eyes and bruises on my left cheek. I cleaned up all the blood and got changed. I booked my ticket for the sea trip to Ancona which I knew would take over twenty hours and then I had to face the prospect of the long journey home. I felt numb and utterly, utterly sad. I could see people staring at me with all the bruises on my face assuming they knew I was involved in some kind of trouble.

My funds were low. I had just enough money for the boat to Ancona. I was thirsty, hungry and very depressed. I was battered and bruised, but my brain was still functioning and I decided to use the cuts and bruises to my advantage. I went to the lost property office on the ship and spoke to the person in charge. Luckily for me, he spoke English. I turned on the tears. With my emotions being in tatters, it wasn't difficult for me and I told him I had been mugged and my wallet had been stolen. He asked me where and when and I told him in Patras earlier that day. "Surely you can see from my bruises that I was badly beaten." I sobbed.

He picked up the phone and rang the purser's office to tell him the story. Within five minutes, the captain came to see me. He gave me a special card with his signature on it that enabled me to eat what I wanted, but no drinks were included and he instructed me that I must eat only at meal times. I ate like a king. I appreciated the offer of food and filled my tray up to capacity with food and plenty of water. When I arrived at the till, the captain was angry as he had told me no drinks. I just turned on the crocodile tears again and he relented. I had to put enough food on my tray to last for a couple of days. I knew I would need it for the long trek home. The sea journey was long and I couldn't sleep, but at least my belly was full. I felt a bit better even though I was sore all over from the beating I had been given. I stayed on the top deck and watched as the ferry took me further and further away from the girl I loved. I couldn't stop thinking about the way I had left her. I was heart-broken, but I determined that I was not finished. I was down, but I wasn't out. After all, I'm a Farnworth lad and I'm English. We don't give up that easily. We fight our corner until we win.

I arrived in Ancona and I thought, my God, I'm thousands of miles from home. The thought was scary, but I simply had to get on my way as best I could. I started to hitch-hike outside the port and when a car stopped, the Italian driver asked in broken English, "Where you going?"

"England," I told him with a smile.

"Ha ha, very funny!" he commented. "Come on, get in. I take you to my house."

Strangely, I didn't feel in any danger. I had just escaped with my life after the worst beating I had ever had, so getting into the Italian guy's car didn't faze me. "I'm Vittorio," he said introducing himself.

I tapped on my chest. "Ian."

We arrived at his house in a matter of minutes and he invited me in to meet his son, Alonso. He also had a daughter who wasn't there at that time. Alonso could speak English and he was very courteous with me. They welcomed me into their home, gave me a sumptuous meal of spaghetti and meatballs, stuffed tomatoes and rice, chips and salads, all washed down with Italian red wine. Vittorio showed me his beautiful garden and invited me to stay the night with them. I told Alonso what had happened to me in Greece and he translated for his father. We spoke until the early hours of the morning. Vittorio reached out and touched my hand and gave me a sympathetic look.

"You must fight for the girl you love and take her to England," Alonso said gently.

I smiled and nodded. "I can promise you," I informed him, "it will take a lot more than a few bruises to stop me getting the girl I love." I had a hot bath and went to bed. I lay awake for a while thinking that I would definitely be back in Greece, but next time I would have a plan of action.

The following morning Alonso told me his father would drive me to the train station and buy me a ticket to Milan. I was to do the return trip to the station where Julie and James had dropped me off just a few days before. When I went into the kitchen, Vittorio's daughter was there and ironically, her name was Maria. However, this Maria was kind and beautiful, not at all like the other one whom I preferred not to think about just then. After breakfast, we had to say goodbye.

As promised, Vittorio drove me to the station, bought my ticket for me and gave me money for food. I hugged him and thanked him. I felt humbled by his kindness. It just proved no matter where you are from, there are some good people in the world.

"Good luck," he said as he left.

I was stuck in Milan for four hours. I kept walking along the main roads out of the city hoping I would be able to hitch a lift. I sat on a bench near a petrol station when a wagon pulled over. The driver must have seen my suitcase and it was obvious I was hitch-hiking.

He pulled in next to me and then wound his window down. He shouted at me in broken English, "Where are going?"

Just like I answered Vittorio, I replied, "England."

He laughed and gestured to me to get in the wagon. I put the suitcase in the back and sat in the front with him. He showed me a map and pointed out to me where he was going - Reims in France. I put my thumb up to him to say that will be fine. It wasn't far from Paris and Paris was a lot closer to home.

It was an interesting journey to say the least. I couldn't speak Italian and his English left much to be desired. The journey took over thirteen hours as we stopped off a few times for something to eat and the driver kindly paid for the food. He didn't tell me his name, but I have to say, he was quite a character. He tried his best to communicate with me and he was a good company. We travelled through Switzerland, Basel, Strasbourg and then on to Reims which was my final destination with him.

He dropped me off on the motorway in the middle of nowhere. It was dark and I was becoming worried because it had been nearly four hours without a lift. Then my knight in shining armour came along. I saw a wagon heading in my direction and he pulled over next to me. And wonder of wonders, an English voice called out, "Where're you going, pal?"

I was so happy. I thought I had won the lottery. "England," I said again.

"Jump in. I'm going to London."

"God is on my side after all," I said to myself.

His name was Albert and he asked me where I had been.

"Greece," I told him. I didn't feel the need to elaborate at that point.

"Were you on holiday?" he asked.

I laughed. "I was only in Greece one day and one night and it had taken me nearly five days to get there."

He looked at me and raised his eyebrows confused. I decided to tell him what had happened in Greece. What harm could it do?

Albert listened and then said, "They're fucking animals them Greeks. You have to watch your back with them."

He was a wonderful character, was Albert. He told me a few stories about what happened on his travels. He told me, once while he was asleep in his wagon in Rome, two guys tried to break into the back of his truck. When he confronted them, they pulled knives on him.

"What did you do?" I asked him.

"I ran like the wind back to the cabin, locked the doors and drove like a bat out of hell until I felt safe."

I tried not to laugh, but he burst out laughing himself so we had a good laugh together. Now and again my thoughts would drift back to Helen and the trouble in the park, but I knew I had been lucky to get out of Greece alive. Next time I had to plan it properly and not just go to Greece on a whim. The trip with Albert was a pleasant and memorable one. We arrived at Dover and then on to London where he dropped me off at a good point on the motorway to give me a better chance of a lift home.

Three or four lifts later, I was in Manchester – home territory- and only a bus ride home to Bolton. I had never been so pleased to see my house. I was so tired, mentally and physically and all I wanted to do was sleep. After a good night's sleep, I got up the following morning eager to start planning my next trip to Athens. I intended to end Helen's nightmare and bring her to England once and for all.

Chapter 2 – The Road to Freedom.

After I settled back into my routine in England, I started my plan to get Helen out of Greece. My first job was to start saving as much money as possible. I had already experienced travelling with very little money and it wasn't easy. I went to the local library to study maps of Greece and plan the best route for our escape. Escape seemed to be a drastic word, but knowing what Helen's family was like, I knew it would be like escaping from jail. In the meantime, I was writing to Helen every day saying how much I loved and missed her and this went on for weeks.

Out of the blue, I received a letter from Helen saying she loved me and missed me and that she was sorry for what her family had done to me. 'Why are you not writing to me?' she wrote. It didn't take a super brain to realise that Maria must have been intercepting my letters and probably having them translated. I decided not to tell Helen my plans to get her out of Greece, or when I was going there. I would make sure Maria knew nothing of my plans, but it meant I had to keep everything secret from Helen too. I continued writing letters to Helen telling her I loved her and missed her and what my life was like in England. As far as Maria was concerned, they were just love letters, but then in one of them, I put in something about Maria and I called her 'a fucking camel.' When Maria intercepted the letter, she was enraged and confronted Helen, telling her what I said. My plan had worked and Helen then knew her mother had been opening her letters.

I received another letter from Helen that confirmed her mother was indeed intercepting her mail and having the letters translated. Helen gave me her friend, Valerie's address, but I had to use a different surname 'Valerie Black' so Valerie would know the letters were from me. I continued to write to Maria's address too so that Maria wouldn't become suspicious. It was becoming like a military operation to get Helen out of Greece.

Gradually, I formulated my plans. I would to fly to Greece and stay for a week, but then travel back by coach with a company called Magic Bus. The Magic Bus was very famous in the nineteen-seventies as a no-frills, cheap way to travel around Europe. The trip would take us through Greece, Yugoslavia, Austria and Belgium. We would catch the ferry to Dover and then finally to London either by train or coach. I decided this was the safest route out of Greece for us. I realised if and when I got Helen, her family or the Greek authorities would be waiting for us at the airport and the ferry port at Patras - the route I had taken after my last trip to Athens. I knew it was dangerous, but when you are in love, you do crazy things. I even bought some clothes to go out in disguise by wearing a cap, dark glasses to hide my face and to dress like the local Greeks by wearing jeans and a light coloured shirt so as not to make it too obvious that I looked like a tourist. Like I said, when you are in love, you do crazy things.

The day before I was due to leave, I went to see my mother and step-dad, Jack. I thought I owed it to them to tell them what I was up to. My mother was very concerned for my safety, but I told her not to worry as I had been planning it for weeks. I spent a short while with them and then I said my goodbyes.

I didn't sleep much during that night. I was thinking about the dangers I might face in Athens, but I had to put bad thoughts out of my head and just concentrate on getting Helen out of Greece. I have to admit I was frightened, not just of her family, but also in case I was unable to see her. However, when morning came, I was ready to go. I was deliberately travelling light in case I had to make a run for it. I arrived at Manchester Airport, checked in my luggage and as I walked through Passenger Control I thought, No turning back now, Ian.

I slept for most of the four hour flight with the help of a sleeping tablet my mother had given me. It stopped me from anticipating what might happen when I arrived at Helen's door. When we landed in Athens, I retrieved my suitcase quite quickly and headed for the exit. I was on the look-out all the time as I going to the bus station. I knew Vangelis and his friends were taxi drivers and did regular airport runs.

I managed to take the bus to Piraeus without being seen, but I needed to find a hotel quickly in case any friends of Helen and her family were around. I was very nervous especially every time I saw a yellow cab. I tried to make sure I was surrounded by people so I couldn't be easily detected. I found the Ionian Hotel on a side street. I felt it would be better for me and out of sight from the main thoroughfare.

I quickly unpacked and went for something to eat, all the time keeping a watchful eye on anyone who might recognise me. My main concern was making sure I wasn't seen. I waited until dark and then I caught the bus to Perama. I got off at the bottom of the hill and waited at the cafe where Helen and I used to drink. Helen had to pass by me if she was going out anywhere. I was drinking coke deliberately to keep a clear head. I didn't want to drink beer. I needed to keep my wits about me. As time passed, Helen was nowhere to be seen. By eleven-thirty it was time for me to go before the last bus left. I got out of the village as quickly as possible, because most of the residents knew me. I was on tenterhooks in case of recognition and I only felt safe when I was back in my hotel.

I did the same thing again the following day and still I didn't see Helen. On the third day I started to panic. I had only a few days left. I had to see her soon otherwise I would have to go back to England without her. I made my way to Perama and did the same thing I had done each day before. I waited in the cafe bar again. At about half-past nine, I saw Helen walking down the hill. My chance at last! I was just going to shout to her when I saw a yellow taxi pass the cafe and Vangelis was driving. Instinctively, I put my head down with my cap over my face. My heart was pounding and I was shaking with fear. I was petrified of being caught, but I was sitting near to the road so Helen had to pass close by me.

When she came near I called her name. She stopped and stood in front of me just staring. I didn't know if she was in shock or if she didn't recognise me. I called out her name again and when I took off my cap and dark glasses, she came straight to me. I held out my hand. She took it and she held on tightly. I left the cafe and I held her tight. She was crying with happiness, but I was very much aware that we had to get out of Perama quickly before we were seen together. We hid in an derelict building off the main road. Out of sight of the world, we held each other, kissed passionately and cried together. I wanted to take her to England and come hell, or high water, I would do just that.

"Do you want to come back to England with me?" I asked longingly.

"Yes, I do," she told me earnestly.

I hugged her tight and I held her in my arms for a few minutes, savouring the moment.

I told her my plans and that we weren't flying back or going via Patras to sail to Ancona. Those would be the first places Vangelis would start looking for us. "We need to travel by coach. Trust me, I have it all planned."

I had to leave, but I told Helen to meet me in my hotel and wear two sets of clothes for the next few days. That way, she would have clothes to take with her. She needed to get her passport, an absolute necessity to get out of Greece. She was fearful of being seen with me as she knew something bad would happen to me if her family caught us together. I reassured her that if we were careful, we would be fine. I kissed her passionately again before I left. She waved to me and left under the cover of darkness.

I walked to the bus stop, caught the bus back to Piraeus and went straight to my hotel. I slept through the night knowing that soon I was going be with Helen and I treasured the thought of being with her always.

The following day, I waited in the hotel for her. When I heard a knock on my door, I was nervous and fearful that Helen had been caught and it would be Vangelis and his cronies. I was in no doubt that in round two, they would finish me off. My fears turned to happiness and relief when I saw it was Helen. I hugged and kissed her. Suddenly, she started to undress and as she took off her clothes she revealed another set underneath. I grinned at her and said, "Well done, my Greek princess! My plan is working." She did the same the next night and afterwards, she gave me her passport. I was delighted that she had been able to smuggle it out of the house without being caught red-handed. We made love for a couple hours which had the desired effect of calming us both down. The next day was judgement day if we were going to get out of Greece safely.

We spoke briefly about that fatal day on the car park. She told me she would never forgive her mother and Vangelis for what they did to me. I told her not to think about it as we still had to get out of Greece.

"Perhaps you had better go home now before your mother starts phoning your friends to find out where you are," I advised her. "We don't want anything to go wrong now that we have come so far. Be here at ten o'clock in the morning. Don't be late, or I will have to catch my flight back to England without you and I don't think I could bear not having you with me." I hugged her and smiled at her affectionately. "Good luck for tomorrow and be extra careful not to get caught otherwise this will be our last chance of being together."

I watched her through the window as she left. My head was swimming with thoughts that it might be the last time I would ever see her. "Please God; let it all go to plan."

I waited till dark and went out for something to eat. I thought a couple of beers might calm my nerves. I covered my movements by going into the side streets thinking, 'Out of sight, out of mind.' I looked around at all the places in Piraeus where Helen and I did our courting. Even though they held very fond memories, I was still glad to be leaving them all behind. Once back in the hotel again, I felt safe, but I didn't sleep a wink. I was more scared than ever, not of being beaten like I had been just a few months before, but of Helen not turning up.

I woke up with a start. It was twenty past nine the following morning. I must have drifted off to sleep and Helen was due in half an hour. My adrenaline was pumping and I could hardly breathe. My nerves were on edge, my knees were shaking and it was now ten o'clock. Every minute seemed like an hour. Twenty past ten and I counted every nervous minute, every frantic second. At ten-thirty-nine, Helen still wasn't there.

I started to panic. What if she isn't coming; what if she's been caught? Then there was a knock on the door. I froze. What if it was Vangelis and his cronies? What if Helen has been caught? I opened the door... it was Helen. I held her as if I had lost her and found her again. I can't describe my relief that she was actually there. All kinds of emotions were running through my mind, but I had to pull myself together. These were my plans and I didn't want to make any mistakes now.

We found the travel company office near to the bus station. We booked two single tickets to England on the infamous Magic Bus. The clerk told us the time of departure and explained the route.

"How long will it take?" I asked.

"It will take four days to arrive in Dover," she told us. "You will need your passports. May I see them, please?"

When she inspected Helen's, she looked up and said, "You will need a visa to travel through Yugoslavia."

My heart sank. "Where do we get a visa?" I asked anxiously. It was a major problem that Helen needed a visa and we needed to overcome that if we were ever going to get to England.

The ticket clerk was very helpful. "Don't worry. Go to the Yugoslavian Embassy in Athens and they will give you a visa. You must go now, because the Embassy will close in two hours. You have time, but remember the coach leaves at four-thirty."

I told Helen not worry. We had to risk getting a taxi, but she was frightened in case Vangelis or any of his friends caught us. "We'll be very careful," I told her, "but we have no choice. We'll have to risk it; otherwise we won't be back in time to catch the coach."

We spotted a taxi driver buying some cigarettes at a kiosk and I asked Helen if she knew him. When she shook her head, I said, "Come on! Quick!" and then to the taxi driver, "Are you free?"

"Yes," he replied. "Where to?"

He took us to the Embassy and outside there were hundreds of people in long lines waiting to be seen. My heart dropped and I said out loud, "We have to get a visa now or we'll miss the coach." As the words came out of my mouth, I noticed a side door open and a security guard came out. I took Helen's hand and said, "This is our chance. You speak to him in Greek. Tell him a sob story; say my father died; anything at all that will help us jump the queue and tell him our coach is leaving in an hour."

Helen worked her magic. To my relief, he let us in. I hugged him and kissed his cheek. I didn't give a damn what it looked like, I was just so happy. We quickly obtained Helen's visa and sped back to the coach before we missed it. The biggest problem now was to get to the coach before the family caught up with us. I knew they would be all over the place looking for us as they had family friends who had taxis and they would stop at nothing to track us down.

We got there with twenty minutes to spare and went to find the Magic Bus. 'Infamous' was the word I used previously and it was indeed the only word to describe it. The windows were filthy and cracked and there were cigarette ends all over the floor. There was no toilet and the back of the coach smelled like a sewer. Helen and I were disgusted and disheartened. The other passengers fitted the brief perfectly. They were either hippies or students who were smoking marijuana, but we had no choice so we jumped on the coach and hugged each other as tears ran down our faces. We had finally made it.

When the coach pulled out of Piraeus, we started out on what promised to be an incredible journey home. I sat back and tried to relax. I was thinking of Maria and Vangelis who would probably be worried about Helen by then and would definitely be searching for her at the airport and at Patras. Maria must have known Helen was with me if she had found out that Helen's passport was missing. I knew I wouldn't feel safe until we reached the Yugoslavian border.

We slept intermittently as we were both mentally and physically drained. Helen slept in my arms. She was totally worn out. We sat near the back of the bus next to a group of lads from Rochdale. Rochdale isn't a million miles from my home town, so I found an affiliation with them. As we approached the Yugoslavian border control, I sensed something unusual was happening. Two Yugoslavian policemen came on board and started to check all the passports. That in itself wasn't strange, but they were armed to the teeth with guns and they looked very intimidating. When it came to our turn, we handed over our passports and I was petrified when he looked at Helen's. I was shit scared! If Maria had reported her missing, we were in deep trouble. The policeman stared first at me, then at Helen. My heart was beating wildly in my chest and I tried desperately not to let the fear show on my face. We waited in silence and then the anguish was over. They returned our passports and walked to the next seat.

Suddenly there was an argument with some of the Rochdale lads, but I was too scared to turn round in case the police thought we were travelling together. The last thing I wanted was any problems with the Yugoslavian police. Two more policemen came onto the coach and walked to the back. The next minute, three of the Rochdale lads were arrested and taken off the coach in handcuffs. I had no idea what was going on, but after a short while the coach was allowed drive over the border and we were on our way.

Once we were out of Greece, we just held each other close and breathed a sigh of utter relief. Giving her a kiss, I said, "Now, we are free! That's the first step on our road to freedom."

After a while, we got to know the Rochdale lads who were still on the coach. They informed us that the three lads who were arrested had been caught with drugs on them. In spite of that, they were all fun to be with and most were in the early twenties. All were characters in their own right. I became friendly with a lad called Jimmy. He seemed to stand out from the rest. He was constantly talking about football violence and the things he used to get up to on his travels following Manchester United. When I told him I hated Manchester United with a passion and we might have crossed swords with each other at some point when we were following our football teams, he asked who I supported.

"Bolton Wanderers, "I told him and he laughed.

"I remember going to Burnden Park," he said still laughing. "It was always a dodgy place to visit."

I laughed with him although I couldn't imagine why Burnden Park would be considered dodgy. It was always a lovely, homely ground. I asked Jimmy what his friends were into in Rochdale.

"Mainly drugs and robbing shops," he said matter-of-factly, "and women," he continued with a wink.

I could see Helen wasn't interested in anything Jimmy had to say, so I ended the conversation with him by making the excuse that Helen wasn't well. We stopped off at various places along the way, some interesting; some not, but the breaks did take our minds off things and it gave us the opportunity to stretch our legs. We drove through Switzerland which was very beautiful and picturesque and then Austria. Eventually after driving for hours we stopped in Brussels in Belgium where we had a four hour break.

Brussels was awe inspiring with each building having unique architectural patterns I had never seen before. I had always been curious about architecture of different countries so I found it very interesting. Helen and I decided to do a bit of sightseeing around Brussels main square as we had plenty of time on our hands. The coach park was close to the square so we didn't have to walk very far. There were charming sidewalks, cafés, shops and restaurants. Helen wanted to go window shopping which we did to pass the time. While we were walking round the shops, we bumped into Jimmy and his friends.

"Do you want to come for something to eat?" he asked. "We can find somewhere and have a drink."

I thought it would do no harm so we followed them into a cafe where we could smell strong coffee and local fish delicacies. Helen and I sat at a separate table and the Rochdale lads sat at two other tables as there were ten of them in all. I picked up the menu and studied the prices. Everything was very expensive, too expensive for me to buy for us both. I knew Helen was hungry and I wanted her to eat. I pretended I had stomach ache and that I couldn't eat much so as not to embarrass myself by not being able to pay the extortionate prices, but I had to make sure Helen had something to eat.

I ordered two coffees and some ham sandwiches for Helen, but I was distracted by the waiters taking lots of drinks and food to Jimmy and his friends. The beer was flowing and they were having a banquet. When I caught Jimmy's eye, he winked at me with a large grin on his face, indicating all the food was on the house. I presumed they didn't have the money to pay for it and it made me feel very uncomfortable. We left the cafe unnoticed by Jimmy and his friends. We didn't want to witness what might happen when they couldn't pay the bill and we decided to make our way back to the coach. As we were walking towards the square, we heard voices behind us. Two of the lads, Mick and Mark had sensibly left the cafe as things were getting out of hand. We hadn't been back in our seats for long, when we heard police sirens. We looked through the coach windows and saw Jimmy and the rest of the Rochdale lads being chased by the police. More and more police arrived in the square and soon all the lads were arrested, handcuffed and put into the waiting police vans.

There were plenty of empty seats at the back of the coach but I have to say, the journey wasn't the same without Jimmy and his Rochdale friends. Helen, who hadn't been impressed by their antics, called the Rochdale lads hooligans. In spite of their being what I would call a rum lot, they had kept us amused during the long journey. The coach set off for Calais, our next stop. It was time to rest. We were tired after the long journey and all the excitement and we slept.

We arrived at Calais, our final destination before we boarded the boat and sailed across the English Channel to England. There was yet another incident with one of the remaining two Rochdale lads. We had changed drivers and the new driver was Greek. I knew there would be problems as Greeks do not like any kind of anti-social behaviour. Unfortunately, Mark was smoking a joint and he was laughing as he urinated on the back seat. I could see the driver looking through his rear view mirror. Helen was disgusted and I had to convince her all English people were not like that. When the coach stopped at the port, the driver complained to the French police and Mark was escorted off and put into a police car.

Soon, we boarded the ferry after our passports had been checked. When we were getting off the coach, Mick whispered to me that when we were in English waters, he would sort the Greek driver out. Once on board, Helen and I headed to the bar. I reckoned I deserved a small beer after all the incidents we had witnessed on our journey. We were chatting when the Greek driver came in, bought a coffee and sat down. Suddenly, Mick, the last of the Rochdale lads ran up to him and knocked him off his chair, knocking him out cold.

It was almost as if Helen couldn't bear any more of the shenanigans and she promptly fainted. I was helping her recover while members of the crew jumped on Mick and frog-marched him out of the bar. I took Helen on deck to get some fresh air and we could see Dover in the distance. I hugged her and whispered, "Soon we will be on English soil and be free." I held Helen in my arms as I stared at the ocean waves. There was something mysterious about staring into the deep waters of the sea. I started to reflect on what had happened in the past few weeks and after all the heartache and tears, love had triumphed in the end. We landed at Dover and we walked down the steps hand in hand onto English soil. I turned to Helen and held her close. "I love you, my Greek princess. Now you are free."

Amidst my happiness, I saw Mick being escorted off the boat by two police officers. I smiled to myself and shook my head slowly. It was the end of an interesting and eventful journey, but for Helen and me, it was the beginning of a new and exciting one.

Chapter 3 – The longest mile is the last mile home...

The long journey from Athens had taken four days. It had been an unforgettable journey full of drama and twists and turns. We were both unbelievably happy. We hugged each other and cried tears of joy and relief when we finally landed in Dover, a major port in England and the gateway to Europe for English people. Now we had to find our way home with very little money. It was four o'clock in the afternoon. The month was October and for that time of year, it was quite mild. I decided we should hitch-hike to London and try to take a coach to Manchester. We didn't fancy hitch-hiking all the way to Manchester. We were desperately tired after the long trip from Greece and we wanted to do the last leg of our journey in comfort. It is said that the longest mile is the last mile home and that's just what it felt like at that time. The fact that we didn't have enough money for the fares would have to be dealt with when we arrived at Victoria Bus Station in London.

We waited on the road out of Dover where I thought it would be easy to get a lift. There had been plenty of wagons on the ferry which I thought would be travelling to different parts of the country. We only waited for about twenty minutes before a wagon pulled up and we got a lift straight away. We were delighted as we were very tired, exhausted in fact from the long, eventful journey from Athens. The driver was going directly to London which was a godsend. We could relax and have a rest without worrying about when we might get our next lift.

The driver was called Charlie. He was a large man with a large, bushy beard and a large smile to match. It was a pleasant journey that took just over two hours. It was rush hour and there was a lot of traffic on the road. Helen slept most of the way so Charlie and I had a good chat about football, my favourite pastime. Charlie was a big West Ham supporter and he told me about his travels round England and Europe.

"I'm a Bolton Wanderers supporter," I told him with a smile. "The furthest Bolton has travelled is to Portsmouth!" which made him laugh out loud. Charlie was good company and a good laugh. He was a typical Cockney character like most of the Cockneys I have bumped into over the years. He even bought us a meal at the motorway services for which we were very grateful.

When we arrived in London, we headed straight to Victoria station where our intentions were to find the National Coaches. Victoria Coach Station is the largest coach station in London and from there coaches travel all over Great Britain and Europe. We needed find a coach travelling north to Manchester. It wasn't difficult. The coach was empty with only the driver on board. I needed to use all my powers of persuasion in order to get him to allow us on board without a ticket. I considered that if I showed him some ID and promised to pay later, he might just allow us to travel.

We tentatively approached the driver. I told him our story which undoubtedly sounded like a sob-story, but it was nonetheless true. When I explained that I had had to smuggle Helen out of Greece, away from her domineering parents so that we could be together, Helen started to weep. "I feel so sick," she wailed. "I'm tired and I'm hungry." We looked earnestly at the driver and waited for his reaction. Praise be to God, the driver took pity on us let us on the coach free of charge. Like I said previously, there are good people in the world and we knew we had been blessed to find several of them in our hour of need.

Most of the journey back, Helen slept in my arms. She was very tired and was more than likely worried about what lay head. She had a lot to face in her new life; a completely different culture. I just relaxed thinking how happy I was, to be with Helen after all the troubles I had faced in Greece. I thanked my lucky stars I had got out alive after taking Maria's daughter away from her family. Rightly, or wrongly, we did what we had to do to be together. I knew her family would be looking for me all over Athens. Their intentions were to get rid of me and they weren't averse to using foul means and evil ways to do it.

We arrived in Manchester at Chorlton Street coach station in the early hours of the morning. To our surprise, before we got off the coach, the Geordie driver whose name was Simon, announced to all the passengers how Helen and I had been forced to escape from Greece and Helen's controlling family so that we could be together. What happened next brought me to tears. Most of the passengers came over and hugged Helen and me. Some had tears in their eyes and they had a collection for us so we could get a taxi home to Bolton from Manchester. We would never be able to thank them enough for their generosity and the seventy pounds they collected was more than enough to get us home in comfort. Good people were appearing everywhere and we were truly grateful. We said our goodbyes to everybody and hugged the driver. "Good luck," he said and we went on our way.

Walking through Chorlton Street bus station was an experience in itself. We passed people who were drunk and sleeping on the litter-strewn floor; tramps drinking bottles of cider ignoring everybody around them. It wasn't a pleasant sight for Helen to see on her first trip to England and I hoped she wasn't wondering what the hell she had come to. She kept her thoughts to herself.

We took a taxi straight to my mother's house in Farnworth just a few miles from Alder Street where I lived. I knew my mother would be waiting up for us as she couldn't wait to see me and especially Helen, whom she felt she knew so much about after the tales I had told her. We arrived at the house and I was so happy and proud of being able to introduce Helen to my mum. When the taxi pulled up outside the house, the light in the kitchen was on. I looked at Helen and she smiled at me and held my hand tightly. She was slightly nervous meeting my mother for the first time, but I reassured her that my mother was gentle and caring and was really looking forward to meeting her.

My mother saw us walking up the path. She had waited up all night to see us. That was typical of my mum. She is the most caring person I have ever met. The door opened and there she was. Her face was a picture. She had tears rolling down her cheeks and I was grinning like a Cheshire cat. She hugged Helen for what seemed ages and she smiled at me as she said, "I'm so proud of you after everything you went through to get Helen here to England. She is so beautiful."

We had a cup of tea and spoke a little about how I managed to get Helen out of Greece. I didn't go into too much detail as I didn't want to frighten her by saying how lucky I was to get out of Greece alive. Helen tried to speak to my mother a little bit, but her English at that point wasn't good. We didn't stay up for long; probably no more than an hour; we were both totally worn out, Helen particularly. She gave my mother a hug and a kiss and wished her goodnight in her cute, broken English.

My mother looked at me and smiled. I think she was so happy and proud. She hugged me and kissed my cheek. I said good night to my mum and took Helen upstairs to the spare bedroom. It was small with a few pictures on the wall and a small dressing table and a wardrobe, but it was warm and cosy. We got straight into bed. I kissed Helen goodnight and I cuddled her until we fell asleep. I didn't think anything about the troubles or the journey home. I just fell into a deep, peaceful sleep.

Chapter 4 – Alder Street and good news!

The following day, we didn't wake up until ten o'clock. We were totally refreshed and after saying goodbye and thanks to my mother and my step-dad, Jack, we were on our way to Alder Street, Great Lever where we would make our new home and our new life together.

Alder Street was a cobbled street with pre-war terraced houses, on each side. The house I lived in was a two-up, two-down house and it belonged to a housing association. It was very modern inside, very spacious with a large front room and modern kitchen. Upstairs were two good sized bedrooms and a small bathroom. It was adequate and it was my home, our home and I intended to make Helen happy there.

I guess this is where the story really begins. I opened my front door and carried her over the threshold as though we were just married. Unfortunately, it turned out to be a bit of an embarrassment as I fell over, unceremoniously dropped Helen on the floor and smashed a Greek vase. Naturally, Helen was a bit shaken, but she burst out laughing. *I hope this is not a sign of things to come,* I thought. I didn't want to think we were already cursed with bad luck.

When I showed Helen round the house, she was delighted. "It's a lovely house," she said happily. "I like it and I'm going to be happy here with you." She settled down quickly. I showed her around the town and the shops and introduced her to a lot of my friends. Her English was improving daily and after a while she felt confident enough to go out on her own. She found out very quickly which shops to go to and she learned which buses to catch. She also learned remarkably quickly about English currency perhaps to my cost.

About eight weeks after we had arrived, she began to feel unwell so I took her to the doctor's. He asked her a few questions about her symptoms and then he examined her, requesting her to provide a urine sample. When she went back into the surgery, he told her he would have to send the sample off to the lab. I was worried there might be something seriously wrong with her, but the doctor informed us. "I think you might be pregnant."

I was in total shock. "She can't be!" I said. "I was in a previous relationship for eight years and nothing happened. We have only been together for a few weeks."

The doctor smiled. "Every relationship is different."

I looked at Helen and she was as white as a sheet. We left the doctor's and walked home. It was not very far and Helen didn't speak a word. When we arrived home, she just put her arms around me and started to cry. I held her in my arms until she was calm. I was in shock too, but the truth of the matter was, I was actually very happy about it. I felt I couldn't show this to Helen as I didn't know what kind of reaction I would get. Looking back, I thought Helen was afraid because her mother used to do everything for her. In Greece, she wasn't allowed to do even the simple things such as ironing, or washing dishes. She was totally under the control of her mother even in things like not being allowed to wear make-up. Her mother had treated her like a child all of her life. She hadn't been allowed to go far from the house and when she did, she had to telephone her mother to say where she was. At twenty years old, I thought it was a bit extreme, but now she was going to be a mother herself and I think the prospect of motherhood daunted her.

I reassured her that everything would be fine and I would always be there for her. My family would help her too and she seemed to calm down. She kissed me warmly and said with a beautiful smile, "I can't believe we will have our own family." It was a magical moment for us both and a special time that we would never forget. We hadn't planned to have a family and for it to happen so soon after Helen's arrival in England was unexpected to say the least.

I smiled at her and told her, "Let's just wait for the results and take it from there."

We decided to keep the news of the pregnancy from my family and friends and for the next few days we carried on as best we could until we got the final results. Four days later, the phone rang. It was the doctor. He spoke cheerily. "The results are here and it's positive. Congratulations!"

The feeling was incredible. I was going to be a father! It was the happiest I had ever felt in my whole life. It was unreal and I said to myself, "My life is going to change forever." The troubles I had in the past were long gone. I went upstairs and told Helen. "You are going to be a mother!" She burst into tears and put her arms around me. This time they were tears of joy.

I rang round all my family, bar my mother and Jack whom I wanted to tell in person. I knew they would be happy with such good news. I decided to go and see them on the same day we had the pregnancy confirmed. I had bought a bottle of champagne the day before. We took a taxi to my mother's house and I had butterflies all the way there. I was so excited to be telling her the brilliant news. When we arrived, we sat in the kitchen and my mother knew straight away I had something to tell her as I couldn't stop smiling. I allowed Helen to break the news as her English was now very good. My mum and Jack were so happy; they jumped up from their chairs and hugged us both fondly.

I looked at Helen and she was really happy. I was very proud of her and I thought she now had a real family who would love her for who she is; a kind, generous and loving girl who had so much love to give. We stayed with Mum and Jack for most of the day and celebrated. It felt the right time and so I got down on one knee. "Helen, will you marry me?"

Helen looked into my eyes and lovingly said, "Yes."

I wanted to tell the whole world that I was going to be a father and I was getting married. I was absolutely ecstatic.

The next four months were spent planning our wedding day. I took Helen into Bolton and walked round the jewellery shops looking for a wedding ring. Next we bought clothes. I found a smart jacket, shirt and tie and Helen bought a purple dress in a size which would disguise her four months baby bump. Over the coming weeks, we ordered the wedding cake and booked everything necessary to give us a wonderful wedding day. On the morning of the wedding in February 1991, I hugged Helen and told her I truly loved her. "Thank you for turning my life around. I would go through all the heartache in Greece again to bring you here. You are the love of my life."

It was just a small affair with a few friends and family at Bolton Register Office. Neither of us wanted too much fuss.

We had a small gathering at our house after the wedding. We cut the wedding cake and celebrated till the early hours. I kissed Helen fondly and I said, "You are finally mine; my Greek princess; my wife who I shall love forever."

Ian & Helen Arrive for their Wedding February1991

Signing the Register - Wedding Day February 1991

It was a wonderful, happy day and one I shall never forget. I married the girl I had fallen in love with on the Greek island of Corfu. I gave Helen an English red rose which I hoped she would keep forever. It was a symbol of our love to remind us that in spite of all the trouble we went through, love conquers all.

Chapter 5 – Building bridges; mending fences.

On the twenty-first of August 1991, two days after the birth of Christopher, I made the momentous decision that we should tell Helen's mother that we were married and had a baby boy. Helen was very reluctant as she has not spoken directly to her mother for almost a year, not, in fact, since that fateful day I smuggled her out of Greece. The only communication she had with her mother was to write to her tell her she was safe in England and that she was living with me, the man she loved and wanted to spend her life with. Helen made sure that she didn't put our address on the letter. We didn't trust her mother, or any other member of her family. We didn't want them to follow us and come to England to reap their revenge.

It was my decision that Helen should tell her mother. I just wanted to put my differences to one side even though I could never forgive her for trying to destroy our relationship. Nor could I forgive her for the beating I received. That said, the day came when Helen plucked up the courage to phone. She was very nervous and very afraid, but she phoned her mother nevertheless. I could literally feel the tension between them. There was a lot of shouting and screaming which went on for a good twenty minutes and then Helen put the phone down. I asked what had happened, and what her mother had said to her. I felt so sorry for Helen. She didn't deserve the way Maria treated her.

She was distraught. She sat down and started to cry. I held her in my arms to comfort her. She was heartbroken and she trembled as I held her close. She had tried to make peace with her mother and all she had received in return was grief. She eventually told me what her mother had said. In a low voice she explained, "All my family and friends, as well as the police had been looking for us all night. They scoured Athens when I went missing with you. My mother and Vangelis even went to Corfu."

"Why did they do that?" I asked unbelieving.

"Because that's where we met and they thought that's where we might go," she told me. "I don't think they could believe I was in England. It is so far away from Athens."

It was apparent that her family had taken drastic steps to find us without success. Helen was twenty years old and they still wanted her to be tied to her mother's apron strings. Things like that should not be happening in the twentieth century. It was strange to me that they hadn't traced us through the ports of exit and entry during our travels. We had used our passports after all, but I realised I was very lucky to escape with my life. Helen was my responsibility now and I would protect her with my life if needs be.

That night we reminisced about much of what had happened to us in the past year. It brought back bad memories of Greece when I first visited Helen in June 1990, when I wasn't allowed to kiss her, or even hold her hand. I remembered on one occasion when Helen and I were kissing like most couples do outside the train station in Piraeus, one of her step-dad's friends saw us and phoned her mother to tell her what he saw. When we got back to the house, her mother slapped Helen and there was a massive argument. There was a lot of screaming and shouting and I felt uneasy and very vulnerable waiting at the top of the steps outside her front door. I didn't want to make the situation worse by getting involved so I kept out of it. In the end, Maria kicked us both out. I wasn't bothered as we stayed together in a hotel in Piraeus and it was a chance to be on my own with Helen without being disturbed. Maria had phoned Helen the following morning, apologising and telling her to come home.

I had to smile. "I'll never forget when we went back the next day," I told Helen. "I had the biggest smile on my face!"

Helen smiled too. "And look at us now," she said. "We have a baby. Maybe that's why my mother shouted at me. We did much more than kissing and holding hands!"

Helen with Baby Christopher

Reminiscing had helped to calm Helen down after the unpleasant phone call. I reassured her that her mother couldn't harm us here in England and anyway, we were married and we had our own life.

A few days later, her mother rang again and this time it was a pleasant phone call which surprised me. Helen told me later her mother had been upset about her leaving Greece the way she did. I found that very strange as Maria had tried everything to destroy our relationship while I was in Athens. I chastised myself. If Maria was trying to build bridges and mend fences, I ought to be more charitable.

Helen said her mum's attitude had changed when she knew she had a grandchild. "Guess what. She wants us all to visit her as a family."

"What a load of bollocks!" I said and Helen understood exactly what I meant as her English was excellent by now.

The phone calls carried on most nights and Helen started to get close to her mother again.

I just let them get on with it. As long as Helen was happy, I didn't mind, but I didn't trust her mother one little bit. We just carried on with our life and I certainly didn't have any intentions of going to Greece again. I didn't fancy waking up in a hospital bed or being found dead on some spare ground in Athens.

Chapter 6 – Facing fears.

It was later in 1991 when we visited her family in Greece. I hadn't even considered going back after the troubles we encountered previously. Helen wasn't nervous at all as she had been in contact with her mother Maria for nearly ten months and they were at peace with each other. It was a different story for me. I was sure Helen's step-father, Vangelis hadn't forgotten the beating he received from me and I certainly hadn't forgotten the beating I received from his family and friends. I tried to convince myself that he would realise I was only defending myself, but I doubted he would understand anything about the emotional and perilous trip to England he had forced me to make without Helen.

On that momentous morning, we set off in a taxi to Manchester airport. As it was six o'clock in the morning, none of us was wide awake so I had Christopher in my arms. There wasn't much conversation between Helen and me. I thought that perhaps it was because it was early in the morning and none of us had much to say at that time of the day. Walking through passport control with Helen and Christopher felt strange. I couldn't put my finger on it, but it was like walking into the unknown. I had resisted taking Christopher to Greece because of my own fears, but I had a very strong feeling inside as if something was going to happen when we arrived.

Helen was quiet throughout the four hour flight. I was quiet too. The nearer we got to Athens, the more nervous I became. I tried to clear all my self-doubts out of my head. I told myself I could deal with anything so long I had my family by my side. I built up my courage with five miniature bottles of vodka. Dutch courage, I know, but I sure felt better with that inside me. I was scared, I admit it. I had been involved in many incidents during my life, some which involved a lot of violence, but I had never been as frightened as I was then.

The plane landed, we collected our suitcases and walked through passport control. In the distance, I could see Helen's mother and step- father waiting for us. My heart sank and my legs were like jelly. I wanted to turn back, but I couldn't. I had two heavy suitcases and anyway, I had to be strong and show no fear. Maria, Helen's mother came over to me and hugged me then Vangelis shook my hand. I was astonished at the reception I received. Vangelis had driven to the airport in his taxi. He put the suitcases in the boot and off we went on a journey to their house in Perama that actually only took just over an hour, but to me, it felt more like six.

I had started to learn Greek to help me know what was going on. I wanted to know everything; what was being said in the conversations between us. We arrived at the house at four in the afternoon. All Helen's family and friends were there. It seemed to be a reception party for us. I picked Christopher up and held him close. I was so scared at this point I thought I was going to die. All kinds of bad thoughts were running through my head. I had had some really bad experiences in Greece with their friends giving me a good hiding, not to mention the death threats from her family which I would not forget in a hurry. Suddenly all her family came over to us. I nearly collapsed. It was like Manchester United fans coming over to me after they had seen my Bolton scarf. I was sure I was going to receive a good kicking, but nothing could have been further from the truth. They actually started to hug me and shake my hand. Phew!

Once we were inside the house, all the family and friends were speaking Greek. Helen reassured me everything was going to be fine and I shouldn't be afraid. Most of her family stayed till the early hours. We had a feast and the drink was flowing. The more I drank, the braver I became. Everybody started to talk to me. I didn't understand what they were saying, but I just smiled and nodded my head as if I understood. It was a very strange atmosphere. I could feel the warmth from them. They were so unusually loveable towards Helen and me.

We stayed for three weeks in all. Everything was fine. We all had a laugh and we forgot about the troubles we had had previously. Helen's family took us everywhere seeing the sights of Athens - the Acropolis, the shops, the harbour and such. As the days went by, Helen's mother and Vangelis were growing very close to Christopher. They loved him and even allowed him to sleep in their bed most nights. They took Christopher with them everywhere in the car. They were just inseparable. I didn't think anything of it at the time. It gave me the opportunity to take Helen out for a few beers and spend time on our own. The three weeks soon passed. It was a great holiday. We had a great time remembering the places where we used to go when I first went over to visit her, especially the Alexandra bar where we did most of our courting.

Maria, Vangelis and Helen playing with baby Christopher

We said our goodbyes at the airport and nearly missed our flight because Maria wouldn't let go of Christopher. She wanted him stay all the summer, but that wasn't going to happen.

We arrived in England very pleased with our return to Greece. We had a great time and I was happy. Helen had made peace with her family and as for me, I managed to forget about the troubles there had been between us.

As the months passed, things in England seemed better. Helen went to college to improve her English. She enjoyed her time there and when she wasn't studying, she socialised and made lots of friends from all around the world. She often went out with them for a drink or a meal. I was happy with that as it gave her break from looking after Christopher. She studied English for a few years and got to the highest grades. Her English grammar was excellent as well as her spoken English which was very fluent.

Christopher was growing up fast and it seemed like only yesterday that he was crawling and saying his first words like Dada. That was one of my proudest moments, hearing him say it for the very first time. I loved every minute I spent with Christopher. I had a very special bond with him since the day he was born. I took on my role not just as a father, but also doing the things normally left to the mother. I enjoyed changing his nappy and feeding him and checking him through the nights whenever he cried. I truly loved Helen, but my love for Christopher was a different kind of love. He was part of me and we had a special bond that I would cherish forever.

Christopher went to the college nursery for the time Helen was at college, but when he was four years old, he went to Saint William of York which was a Catholic school in Great Lever and was just five minutes from where we lived. We visited Greece nearly every year and sometimes three times a year depending on our finances. I truly loved Greece. It had a special place in my heart, because it was where I met Helen. Troubles apart, Greece will always have a special place in my heart.

However, the more times we went to Greece, the closer Maria and Vangelis would be to Christopher. I remember on various occasions Maria asking Helen, "Why don't you leave Christopher in Greece? We would love to raise him. He would be so happy here." More than once she told Helen that she would be much happier without all the worries and stresses of raising a child. I thought nothing of it at the time. I just thought she was having a bit fun with Helen. I ignored the fact that Maria took over the role of being Christopher's mother whenever we went to Greece - changing his nappies, bathing him, feeding him. Helen didn't seem to mind as she was having a break and a rest. As well as that, Vangelis would take him everywhere in his taxi when he was not working. He truly loved Christopher like his own son as he told me often enough. Naïve as it may appear, I thought at the time it was just a natural thing as he didn't have any children of his own.

When we were in England, Maria would often ring us and ask us to send him over for a few months. I always objected, not because I didn't trust her with him, but because I couldn't bear the thought of being apart from my son for so long. This went on and on for a long time, year after year. Eventually, Maria got the message as I told her straight it would never happen.

Helen, Christopher and I went to Spain a few times over the next few years much to the annoyance of Maria. She felt we should go to Greece all the time, but we did make the effort to go out to Greece when we could and they were all great times.

When Christopher started school, he was four years old. I was working five days a week and Helen had finished her college exams and passed them all. I was very proud of her and she eventually went on a training course to become a secretary at Bolton Market Radio, working for Dorothy, who was in charge of the operation there. I became very good friends with Dorothy and her husband Alan. Market Radio was a charity and training organisation to help people who were low on confidence. They also gave opportunities to people with disabilities to learn about computers and give them a chance for a qualification in how to train in radio broadcasting. Dorothy and Alan did a lot of charity work in Bolton. They gained a lot of recognition and well-deserved too.

In February 1994, I wrote a love story and won a competition in the Bolton Evening News. The prize was a trip to Paris for a Valentine's break. I wrote about how I met Helen and how I fell in love on a Greek Island; how I smuggled her out of Greece and got married.

We invited Helen's mother to England to look after Christopher so she could spend some precious time with him while we were away in Paris.

Paris was a great experience. It was Valentine's Day while we were there so I made it a special occasion for Helen. We went on a boat trip on the River Seine and had a Valentine's meal on the cruise boat. It was very romantic especially when we walked along the river bank in the moonlight and visited the Eiffel Tower. Paris was a fantastic trip and it will always be a special memory that I was in the city of romance with girl I truly loved.

When we arrived back in England to Alder Street, Christopher was so happy to see his mummy and me. He was very excited. He had missed us so much and he couldn't stop giving us both cuddles. I was quite shocked that Maria did something I didn't immediately understand. She went upstairs and came back down with her suitcase. She was extremely jealous that Christopher was paying us so much attention on our return.

"Why is he all over you two?" she asked. "I have looked after him while you were away in Paris and now he doesn't want me anymore. It's not fair after the time I have spent with him." She was sulking like a spoilt child.

I tried to explain to her that we were his parents and it was normal to miss us when we had been away. If she had stamped her feet in a tantrum, I wouldn't have been surprised, but she told Helen she wanted to go to stay with Auntie Maro who lived in Aston-in-Makerfield. Helen and I had stayed with her on occasions. "Call me a taxi, Helen," Maria demanded. "I won't stay here any longer. I'll stay with Auntie Maro until I go back to Greece." When the taxi arrived, she went off in a huff. I was pretty annoyed at her attitude. She was showing her true colours and I thought she was very childish.

"I can't believe your mother just did that," I said to Helen when she had left. "She's pathetic! What does she expect? Christopher was bound to be pleased to see us. He's our child, not hers and the sooner she realises that, the better."

Helen agreed.

I didn't see Maria again after that. For the last few days that she was in England, she stayed in Aston-in-Makerfield. Helen took Christopher to see her on one occasion, but I stayed away as I was still annoyed with her attitude and self-pity. I had no time for her self-centred behaviour.

We didn't return to Greece for four years. I had no intentions of putting up with Maria's stupidity. She still rang Helen every week and still tried to dictate what she should do with her life. Most annoying for me was the fact that she still went on about Christopher going to Greece for holidays, but her requests fell on deaf ears. There was no way I would allow it.

Chapter 7 – Influences from afar.

One morning Helen received a phone call from her mother, Maria, to tell her that her grandma had died. "You have to come to Greece for the funeral," her mother cried. "You have to, Helen."

Helen was heartbroken. Her grandma had helped to raise her from a young age while Maria followed her husband, Helen's father, around Greece as he was touring with a band.

Later, Maria had divorced Helen's father and remarried Vangelis and they had been together for a number of years. Helen never saw much of her real father as he never really bothered with her for reasons of his own. To Vangelis' credit, he took Helen on as his own daughter and supported her. He paid her college fees and made sure she had everything she needed.

Helen cried for most of the day and night. She was completely overcome with grief. "My grandma was like a mother to me. I have to go and pay my last respects, Ian. Please say I can go."

I went into Bolton the following day and booked a flight to Athens for her. She was going for two weeks, but she was travelling on her own. On the morning she left, she told me she loved me and would miss me. She said goodbye to me and she hugged Christopher before she left in a taxi to go to the airport.

For the first few days after she arrived in Greece, she rang me quite frequently, but as the days went by, the phone calls became fewer and fewer. I didn't suspect anything was wrong as I thought Helen was just upset over her grandma's death. The two weeks went by fairly quickly. Christopher was contented and settled even though his mother was in

Greece. I kept him well occupied by taking him out every day and by taking him to the cinema and visiting my family.

When Helen arrived home, it felt almost as though she had never been away. Strangely though, she was not the same girl when she came back. She was very nervous and a bit distant with me. We didn't kiss much, or cuddle and that was odd because we were usually all over each other. Conversations dried up and she seemed to be deliberately keeping out of my way most of the time. Her sulky mood lasted for two days before she said something I didn't expect.

"I want to go back to Greece and take Christopher with me," she said confidently.

"What?" I asked dumbfounded at what she had announced.

"I want to go for the whole summer," she continued, "just Christopher and me."

I was quite taken aback, "Why do you want to go on your own with Christopher?" I asked. "Why can't I come too?"

She couldn't look me in the eye and give me a straight answer. She was obviously worried what my reaction would be, because she knew my answer before I actually said it. "There is no way Christopher is going to Greece for all that time without me. Apart from missing him too much, you are depriving me of being with him." I was very angry with her for even suggesting they should go to Greece without me. She knew how close to Christopher I was and separation would be too much for us both. Christopher and I went everywhere together, most times with Helen too, because we were a family.

I took hold of her arms and held them tightly. I was shaking her, not violently, but showing how serious I was and asking what was wrong with her. I tried to reason with her, but she just wouldn't listen to me or give me any answers. I was really angry and frustrated with her so I just walked away into the kitchen to calm myself down. It was something new to me as Helen and I had never argued with each other We were just so close, but I realised she had probably been influenced by Maria and Vangelis while she had been in Greece. I knew they would try to convince her she should go back to live in Greece and take Christopher with her.

I sat quietly in the kitchen for a while in order to collect my thoughts. I didn't often lose my temper, but at that point I had been beside myself with rage. I was just glad Christopher was at school. I didn't want him to see his parents arguing. It was something I experienced with my own parents when I was younger and I didn't want Christopher to feel like I did during those times.

Helen just grabbed her coat and stormed out of the house. I had no idea where she was going and I didn't see her for most of the day. I thought she might have been at the school to pick up Christopher at three-thirty, but she wasn't there. I was getting worried because she didn't ring me or do anything to let me know where she had gone. Christopher was asking where his mother was and I just told him she was at his grandma's. I didn't want to upset him by saying I didn't know where she had gone.

Christopher watched television for a while before I made his favourite tea – chips, fish fingers and beans. When it was time for bed, I read his bedtime stories and kissed him good night. By seven o'clock, I still hadn't heard from Helen. I rang my mother to see if she had gone there and just made the excuse that she may be calling to see her. I didn't want to worry my mother. I needed to sort it out myself.

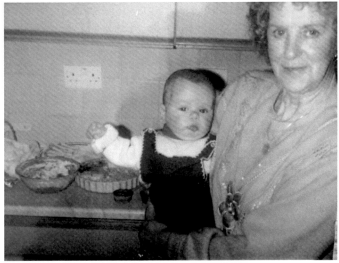

Ian's mother with baby Christopher

At nine o'clock, Helen returned. She just walked in and went straight to bed without saying where she had been or trying to clear the air. The following morning, she carried on with the silent treatment. She refused to say why she wanted to go Greece with only Christopher. Finally she just came out with it. "I want a divorce."

To say I was in shocked is an understatement. I just stared at her.

"I've already seen a solicitor. That's where I went yesterday if you're interested," she said with venom in her tone.

I was totally devastated. I burst into tears. My emotions were in turmoil. "Why?" I asked, "Why are you are breaking my heart? Why, Helen, why?"

"I miss my country and my family and I want to go home with Christopher," she told me.

I tried to hold her in my arms, but she pushed me away. "Please don't leave me, Helen," I begged. "I love you."

She turned away from me and went upstairs. I sat down with my head in my hands and wept until I could weep no more. I looked at the pictures on the wall, pictures of the three of us, our family portrait. I couldn't believe my marriage was coming to an end. I just couldn't bear to be without Helen and Christopher. They were my whole life.

I left the house in tears and I went for a walk to clear my head. I sat in the park near my house for over two hours not realising how the time passed as I stared into space seeing nothing, but the visions of all I had gone through to bring Helen to England. I went back to the house and I begged her again, but I received the same answer.

"It's over between us and I won't change my mind."

When Helen went to pick Christopher up from school, I decided I had no choice but to make an appointment with a solicitor for the following afternoon. I had never seen Helen so determined before. She had always looked to me to make the decisions. I was like a zombie. I couldn't believe I was losing the girl I truly loved after everything we had been through. I reluctantly decided it must be over between us. I had no fight left in me at that point. I had never seen this side of Helen in all the time we had been together.

When she returned home with Christopher, I told her that Christopher would never go to Greece without me. Her face was distorted, she was so angry. I just couldn't understand any of it. As far as I could see, I had done nothing wrong. I only ever gave her my love.

For the next few nights we slept apart. We didn't speak even though I tried. She was a different girl, not the Helen I knew; the Helen who had been so loving and caring. On the morning I was going to see my solicitor, I begged her to change her mind. "I love you so much, Helen. Why are you so hell bent on hurting me?"

I informed her I was seeing a solicitor that morning and I was going to apply for custody of Christopher. She walked away from me saying nothing and I just left, banging the door shut. I did it with such strength, it nearly came off its hinges, but it released the tension I was feeling. As I headed into town, I felt numb. I was in tears on the bus and I didn't care who was looking at me. I wasn't in control of my emotions and I just let the tears flow. When I saw my solicitor and told him what was happening, he advised me that I must sign papers to get an injunction to stop Helen from taking Christopher out of the country. I was going to sign the papers, but I received a phone call from Helen, begging me not to go ahead with the divorce. She told me she was sorry and she still loved me. I had to tell the solicitor I had changed my mind, but he advised me to sign the papers anyway. I refused on the grounds that I loved her and she loved me. I just got up and left.

I met Helen in town and when she saw me she hugged me and started to cry. She said she was sorry and begged for forgiveness. I just hugged her and held her in my arms tightly I was so relieved the nightmare was over and we were back together. I asked Helen not to mention about the arguments and the threat of divorce to anybody. It had to remain in the past and we needed to get back to what we were like before - loving and caring.

The next few months were fantastic. Helen seemed to be her old affectionate and caring self and all the doubts I had, disappeared. In June 1998 we went on holiday to Cyprus for a week. We stayed in Paphos which is the best known resort on the Cyprus west coast. A traditional harbour town, it had a handful of golden beaches and a pretty marina and a long list of historical sites, including the Tombs of the Kings. I loved it; we loved it. Cyprus was a very beautiful island and it was the first time I had visited. Occasionally Helen would ring her mother and when she came back her head was sometimes in the clouds, her mind elsewhere. When I asked her what was wrong, she just said she was tired and that was that. I never suspected anything at that time. I believed everything she said because I was so in love with her. To my mind, she could do no wrong.

Much as I enjoyed the holiday in Cyprus, it was not like all the other holidays we had. I couldn't explain it. Helen was up and down each day, sometimes she was caring and fun to be with, other days she was quiet and moody. I put it down to her being tired some days, or maybe it was just a woman thing. I really didn't know what she was thinking, or if she had something on her mind that was worrying her. In hindsight, maybe my love was blind, but I trusted her and believed what she was telling me.

Chapter 8 – Hell hath no fury like a woman on a mission.

When we arrived back in England from our holiday in Cyprus, life wasn't the same. Helen hadn't been excited about it at all like she had been during our previous holidays. She was polite and still caring, but seemed tired and miserable all the time, a bit lethargic and she walked around as though she had the worries of the world on her shoulders. When I asked about it, she said the same thing over and over again. "Stop worrying, Ian. I'm just a bit tired sometimes."

"But I do worry about you," I told her. "I don't like the thought of you being tired all the time. We've just had a lovely holiday in Cyprus so you should be feeling a little bit refreshed at least."

It seemed the holiday was soon forgotten as we both went back to work and Christopher went back to school. Helen still received phone calls from her mother in Greece. I didn't get involved in the conversations with Maria because she and I didn't have much to say to each other. On one particular weekend, I thought it would cheer up Helen if I took her out for a treat. I had already arranged for Christopher to sleep over at my mother's house so finding a babysitter wasn't a problem. We went to Wetherspoon's in Bolton for a pub meal and a drink.

I had steak and chips with mushrooms and onion rings followed by ice cream. Helen had plaice and chips with vegetables. They were good old fashioned Lancashire meals that always tasted good when you haven't had to make the food yourself. We had a bottle of red wine too. It felt very romantic. We held hands across the table and occasionally she gave me a kiss.

For me it was like when we first met, but out of the blue she asked, "Why don't we go to Greece for a couple a weeks and stay with my mum? She will look after Christopher and we can go out every night like this and relax and have a good time. We both need to relax more."

"We'll see," I replied. Committing to another trip to Greece at that point hadn't been on the agenda,

For the next few days, she kept on asking me to take her to Greece. She was using all her feminine wiles on me and I gave in. I couldn't resist her when she came on to me with that passionate look in her eyes and her seductive touch. The following day, I took her to the travel agents and booked our flights. We would go to Athens for two weeks. Helen was so happy. She knew how to win me over.

Two weeks before we were flying out, Maria phoned Helen every night and stayed on the phone for over an hour sometimes. It was my considered opinion that Maria was excited about seeing Helen and Christopher. I understood that. I took Christopher to see his grandma, my mother and she asked me where Helen was. "I haven't seen her for ages."

"She's got a bad stomach," I lied. "She daren't leave the house in case she needs the toilet urgently."

As I was leaving, my mother just came out with it. "What's the real reason Helen hasn't come tonight? She can't have had a bad stomach for the last few weeks. Is there anything wrong?"

I shook my head. "Nothing wrong," I told her. "Don't worry about us. We are fine."

"Whatever you say, Ian," Mum said, "But just watch yourself in Greece. I really don't trust that Maria woman."

"Stop worrying, Mum," I told her again. "Everything will be fine."

When Christopher and I arrived home, we all had an early night. We were flying very early in the morning and we had to be at the airport for four o'clock. I tried to sleep, but I couldn't. Helen was awake too, just staring at the walls as though she was in a trance. Eventually, I fell asleep and it was Helen who woke me up packing the suitcases.

"What are you doing?" I said sleepily. "I thought you had already done the packing."

"I forgot to put pack a few things which Christopher will need," she told me. "He's a child. He'll need lots of clothes while we are away."

When taxi arrived, I picked up the suitcases and both of them were very heavy, much heavier than usual. "What the hell have you put in these cases, Helen?" I asked puffing and panting from the effort. "We'll have to pay excess luggage at the airport if they are too heavy and that isn't cheap."

Helen just shrugged and said nothing.

The taxi driver helped me put the cases in the boot and I went back into the house to get Christopher. Helen was standing silently in the front room, staring around at everything. I noticed she was upset. "What's wrong, love?"

"I always get upset when I go to Greece,' she told me.

"Our home will still be here when we get back," I said smiling. I put my hand on her arm. "We have to go. The taxi is waiting."

As the taxi was leaving, Helen turned round and stared at our house and the street. I found it a bit strange, but because I was preoccupied with Christopher, I didn't think about it afterwards. Only now as I write have I realised the reason behind her actions.

The flight seemed longer than usual this time and Helen, for reasons best known to her, was very quiet. We all slept for most of the flight as we were all very tired having been up at four o'clock in the morning. The flight arrived on time and we didn't wait too long to go through passport control which was usually a nightmare with the Greeks, as they were notoriously slow. I collected the suitcases and I still thought they were heavier than usual. Helen's mother and Vangelis were there to pick us up. This time the greeting was cool to say the least. There was no sign of friendliness or affection like there had been the last time we visited them. This time, even though they were still pleasant enough towards me, they didn't have a lot to say and something was different.

We arrived at the house in the usual time it took from the airport, but there were none of the relatives or friends there to greet us. Everything was subdued and I felt there was a very strange atmosphere. As the days went by Helen didn't want to go out with me at all. I didn't understand what was going on even though I felt everything was strange. Helen's mother and Vangelis just took control of Christopher. They wouldn't allow me take him out of the house. Their excuse was, it was too hot for him.

Hindsight tells me I was completely naïve, but I ignored what was happening. I didn't want to rock the boat. The first week went by and Helen still wouldn't go out of the house with me.

"When I agreed to come out here, you said we would be able to go out and have some fun and relaxation," I reminded her. "We've been here a week and you've not wanted to do anything. What's wrong with you? We are on holiday for goodness sake."

Annoyingly, she kept coming out with the same excuses. "I don't feel well because of the hot weather. It makes me feel tired all the time after all the cold weather in England."

"Well, I hope you'll feel better soon," I said, "because I would like to go out during my holiday; maybe tomorrow?"

"Maybe," she said showing very little interest.

I sighed. I just wanted to spend some time with my wife, but she wasn't playing and I allowed her to wallow in her selfishness, because I loved her and wanted to please her without causing a row.

I went out to Athens a few times on my own. I loved the Acropolis and I visited it every time I went to Greece. I also visited a few more tourist places, hit a few bars and had a few drinks. The holiday was already into the second week and still Helen wasn't making it easy to relax. She was very quiet, not her normal chatty self. I tried to find out was wrong with her, but she just kept saying the same old things. "I'm not well; I'm tired," and I let her get away with it.

Her mother and Vangelis were always with Christopher and I still didn't really latch on to what was happening, although I did complain to Helen. When I did tell her how I felt, she told me it was all in my head. "They are always with him," I complained. "He's my son and they don't allow me to spend any of my holiday time with him. They are in control and I don't like it."

"They are not controlling him," Helen argued. "They are just showing him love and affection while he's here. They haven't seen him for a long time, Ian. Stop moaning about it."

"Well, you come out with me then," I suggested.

"All right if it will stop you complaining," she said.

We went to the Alexandra bar where we did all our courting during my first ever visit to Greece. Helen was still not very talkative at all. She seemed to be miles away, her head was somewhere above the clouds and it was as if I wasn't there with her. She spoke very little, but then she asked me, "Ian, do you love me? Would you ever come to live with me in Greece?"

"I love you very much," I told her, "but we can't live in Greece. I have a job in England, our house is there and Christopher's school is there. We can't live here in Greece without the security of a job and money and a house."

She went very quiet again and her mood changed. She was like that the whole holiday. I began to grow a bit suspicious, but not enough to realise what was going on. I couldn't help thinking about the evil side of Maria and Vangelis. I was only too aware of their past controlling of Helen and they seemed to be trying the same ploy with Christopher. I just wanted to get this holiday over with and go home. I thought about challenging Maria and Vangelis, but I didn't want the situation to get any worse than it was already. I was in their house. I had no control and I was afraid if they kicked off with me, it could escalate into the violence I had personally experienced before. I was determined that I wouldn't involve Christopher in any trouble, so I decided to turn a blind eye till we all went back home to England.

With all that was going on, I had already decided that I wouldn't go back to Greece again. I hated the unfriendly atmosphere and not going out around Athens like Helen and I used to do. Maria and Vangelis were not as warm and welcoming as they had been on our other holidays. Surely they should have realised how much I loved Helen and I didn't want to keep arguing with her and challenging what was going on. I was frightened of losing her and thought that if I couldn't get along with her parents, it would be very difficult for us both, but Maria and Vangelis did nothing to encourage a pleasant relationship for any of us. I was deeply in love with Helen from the start and as far as I was concerned, I always would be.

With only three days of the holiday left, Christopher's birthday was approaching. On the day of his birthday, I went into Athens on my own to buy him a birthday cake and a few toys for his presents. When I returned, Maria and Helen were getting the food ready for the party which had previously been a big occasion when we were in Greece on his birthday. By evening, I was getting excited for Christopher as he was looking forward to his presents like all little boys do. I noticed there wasn't as much food on the table as usual - just his cake and a few sandwiches. "How many people are coming?" I asked.

"Just us and a couple of friends," she replied.

"How come?" I asked without hiding my surprise. "We usually have a big do for Christopher's birthday," but before she answered, there was a knock on the door. Helen's Auntie

Rula and her son came in and I asked Helen again, "Who else is coming?"

"That's it," she replied.

"How come?" I asked again. "Usually nearly all the village turns out. Why not this time?"

Birthday Boy Christopher

She shrugged her shoulders, walked away and sat down at the table with her auntie.

Maria and Vangelis soon followed her and sat down with them. It was a very mundane affair, miserable in fact. I sat there and nobody took any notice of me. Christopher, however, was getting excited opening his presents. I was happy for him, but I was feeling very depressed about the holiday. The family made me feel as though I didn't exist. I felt extremely uncomfortable about the whole situation. To complain to them might open the flood gates and I was severely out-numbered. It just wasn't worth the risk. The party was over quickly. Helen's Auntie Rula left with her son after a very short time. The night was over before it had begun. I felt so sorry for Christopher. I wanted it to be a big occasion for him. Thankfully, he was oblivious to what was going on around him. He was only seven years old and he had presents so he was happy. Helen went to bed early; so did Vangelis and Maria. It was eleven o'clock and usually the party would have been an all-nighter. I just didn't understand what was going on at all. I went and sat outside on the balcony for a few hours. I had a few beers. I was so upset and I just wanted to go home. I had no intentions of ever going back to Helen's parents' house again.

At that time, I began to understand how people suffering from depression must feel. I was looking up at the sky, gazing at the stars, lost in the blackness that enveloped me. Tears were rolling down my face and I felt so alone. I loved Helen so much yet I felt she was deeply sad with her life. I could see it in her eyes; I could feel it when she was around me, yet I was too frightened to challenge her. I had been so hurt when she wanted to divorce me. The pain I felt was like a knife going through my heart. I knew there was something wrong during our time in Cyprus and Greece, but I was so frightened of finding out the truth. I was so besotted with her. We had been through so much together and to lose her would be devastating so I decided to ignore everything that was going around me. I just wanted to go home, just the three of us – Helen, Christopher and me. I knew I had only a couple of days to put up with what was going on and it wouldn't be long before we would be on our own, away from the clutches of Maria and Vangelis.

Alone in Athens

When I went to bed, Helen was fast asleep. Christopher was sleeping with Maria. I held Helen in my arms and I whispered to her that I loved her and that I could not live without her. With that I went to sleep, but I remember waking up in the morning and seeing Helen standing at the bottom of the bed just staring at me and then she went away without saying anything. When I was dressed, I found Maria in the kitchen. "Where is Christopher?" I asked.

"Helen has taken him for an ice cream," she told me.

I was curious, but I just looked at her and went into the bathroom for a wash and shave. I heard the telephone ringing and Maria shouted that Helen wanted to speak to me. I picked up the phone and it was then that I received the bombshell!

"Ian, I am not coming back to England and Christopher is staying here with me," she said.

I suppose I shouldn't have been shocked after recent events, but I was. "Not all this again," I exclaimed. "Please Helen don't leave me. I love you. How many times do I have to tell you? Christopher is my son; he's my life; please don't take him away from me..." Before I could finish what I wanted to say, she put the phone down.

Instantly I felt sick to my stomach. I was shaking and I had to go to the toilet where I promptly vomited. When I came out of the bathroom, I was in tears. Maria was standing next to the door. It was open and she snarled at me, "Leave." She threw my suitcase down the stairs. "It's finished; it's over. You will never see your wife and child again."

I looked at Maria with devastation in my eyes. I felt so empty inside and I didn't have the strength to fight back anymore. I walked down the steps a broken man, holding a suitcase. I had nowhere to go and I could only see a lonely, uncertain future ahead of me.

Chapter 9 – I will not go down without a fight.

I was crying all the way down the hill from her house, a hill that held so many memories for me. I tried to blank them out, but a man who had just been dealt the hand I had, really thought that life was not worth living. I walked past the cafe bar at the bottom of the hill where I was once waiting with so much hope of taking the girl I loved back to England with me. It all seemed so long ago; a beautiful dream that had turned into a nightmare.

I sat on a bench with my head in my hands. I just wanted to die. Life had no meaning anymore. People were passing me by, but I was oblivious of everyone around me. Yet, from somewhere deep inside, I knew I had to find the strength to fight for my boy and my love for Christopher would sustain me in whatever I had to do.

I made my way into Athens by taxi. I headed for the British Embassy. I needed help and advice. I walked through the main doors and was stopped by a security guard. "You need an appointment to see someone," he told me.

I looked at him in desperation. "Please," I begged. "I have to speak to somebody. My son has been stolen..." I couldn't speak properly through my tears. "Please," I sobbed. "Please let me speak to somebody who can help me." My voice grew stronger and more demanding. "I want my son back. Please help me."

The security guard left and within a few minutes he returned with an official who spoke English. He took me into a side room and I told him what had happened.

The official understood the situation and said the words I wanted to hear. "She cannot take your child. It is kidnapping. Let me have the telephone number and I will speak to her."

Maria answered the phone. "I am calling from the British Embassy in Athens. I need to locate the whereabouts of the child, Christopher Lomax."

"I don't know where he is," Maria answered.

"Where is Helen Lomax?" the official asked and again Maria said she didn't know.

I could hear the conversation throughout and Maria lied through her teeth. "Helen and Christopher have gone away because Ian Lomax has been beating them."

"She's lying," I whispered. "I love them both very much."

"You could be charged with kidnapping if you don't bring the child back to his father..." the official informed Maria bluntly, but Maria put the phone down and cut the conversation short.

He looked at me and I could see the sympathy in his expression. "For the record," he said, "I don't believe what she is saying. You must go to the police and tell them what has happened. I'm sure they'll look into the kidnapping situation. Don't leave Greece because your wife could say you abandoned her and your child."

I hoped the Greek police would lay the kidnapping charges so that I could go home and find myself a good lawyer. The Embassy official explained that a lawyer would apply to the Lord Chancellor's Office in order for me to take Christopher home to England under the rules of the Hague Convention. The Hague Convention 1980 dealt with the civil aspects of international child abduction. It is a multilateral treaty, which seeks to protect children from the harmful effects of abduction and retention across international boundaries by providing a procedure to bring about their prompt return.

I needed to return to Perama where Helen lived and try to find Christopher before it was too late. She had stolen Christopher the day after his seventh birthday, the day we were supposed to be flying home. I realised she had been planning it for months with Maria and Vangelis. I felt so stupid and I was angry with myself for not seeing the signs right in front of me. I had allowed my heart to rule my head. I was completely oblivious to her devious actions; blinded by love.

I thought back to the time she had gone to Greece for her grandmother's funeral. It must have all started then. Helen tricked me into stopping the divorce after I threatened to apply for custody of Christopher in my own country and the country of his birth. She was cunning; I could see that now. I looked back to our holiday in Cyprus when her mind was elsewhere. I should have known then and she tricked me into going to Greece so she could put her foul plans into action and steal my child. I felt no love for her anymore; only anger and hate. She didn't love me, but I would never give up my fight for Christopher.

I searched high and low for them, going to a friend's house in Malpos and to Valerie's house. None of them had seen Helen and Christopher. I went to the park where I used to take Christopher, but I couldn't find them anywhere. In my despair, I knew he was gone and I thought I would lose him forever. I made my way to the police station in Perama, not far away from Maria's house. I needed to report what had happened. The police sergeant on the reception desk listened as I told him. I broke down in tears. I just could not take any more pain and suffering.

The police officer came from behind the desk and put his hand on my shoulder. "I'm Remanos," he said gently. "What's their telephone number?" He was a caring man who spoke in broken English. He had short, black hair and sported a small moustache. He wasn't very tall as policemen usually are, but he inspired me with confidence because he was so friendly.

"I'm Ian," I told him as I gave him the number and he dialled.

I could hear Maria's voice. Remanos was shouting at her. I could understand a few words of Greek and he was telling her she was going to be charged with kidnapping unless she brought Christopher to the police station. Maria put the phone down and Remanos was not at all pleased. He brought in another police officer to translate for me as he explained what I had to do to charge Helen with kidnapping. I signed the papers and they would in turn be served on Helen. That done, Remanos asked me when I was due to go back to England?

"I'm due to fly out at two o'clock in the morning," I told him.

He put his hand on my shoulder again. "You stay here until it is time to leave," he suggested. "I will take you to the airport myself. It's for your protection, you understand." He left the room for a few minutes then came back with a bottle of coke. He looked and smiled at me. "Sorry I can't offer you anything stronger," he said laughing.

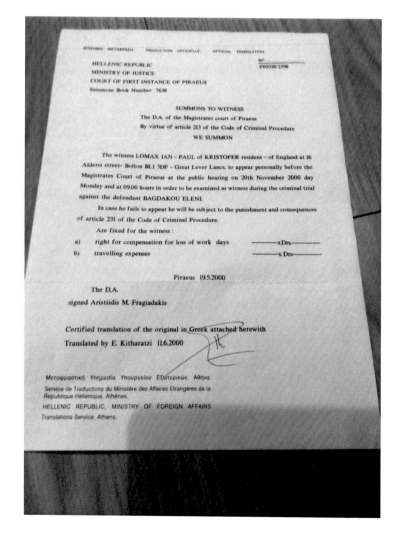

EΠΙΣΗΜΗ ΜΕΤΑΦΡΑΣΗ   TRADUCTION OFFICIELLE   OFFICIAL TRANSLATION

N°
F09318/2398

HELLENIC REPUBLIC
MINISTRY OF JUSTICE
COURT OF FIRST INSTANCE OF PIRAEUS
Summons Book Number 7638

SUMMONS TO WITNESS
The D.A. of the Magistrates court of Piraeus
By virtue of article 213 of the Code of Criminal Procedure
WE SUMMON

The witness LOMAX IAN - PAUL of KRISTOFER resident - of England at 16 Alderst street- Bolton BL1 3DF - Great Lever Lancs, to appear personally before the Magistrates Court of Piraeus at the public hearing on 20th November 2000 day Monday and at 09.00 hours in order to be examined as witness during the criminal trial against the defendant BAGDAKOU ELENI.

In case he fails to appear he will be subject to the punishment and consequences of article 231 of the Code of Criminal Procedure.

Are fixed for the witness :

a)   right for compensation for loss of work days   ———xDrs.———

b)   travelling expenses   ———x Drs———

Piraeus 19.5.2000

The D.A.

signed Aristiidis M. Fragiadakis

Certified translation of the original in Greek attached herewith

Translated by E. Kitharatzi 11.6.2000

Μεταφραστική Υπηρεσία Υπουργείου Εξωτερικών. Αθήνα.
Service de Traductions du Ministère des Affaires Etrangères de la République Hellénique. Athènes.
HELLENIC REPUBLIC, MINISTRY OF FOREIGN AFFAIRS
Translations Service. Athens.

"No problem," I said, "and thanks." At that moment I made a friend and I knew I would see him again whenever I had to be in Greece. "Next time I'll bring you a bottle of whiskey," I told him, "and we'll have a drink together."

He nodded, but then our conversation was interrupted by loud shouting outside. From where I was sitting, I could see Vangelis in the reception area. Remanos left me and went outside. I could hear him shouting and see him waving his arms at Vangelis, but the confrontation didn't last long before Vangelis walked away.

"That big brute was trying to stop you laying charges for kidnapping," Remanos explained. "He was saying you have been beating your wife and your child, but I told him to clear off. He's a liar; I can tell a liar a mile off!"

"Thanks, Remanos. I appreciate your help," I told him genuinely.

"I have a child too," he said, "but my wife and I are separated. Mind you, we don't have the problems you seem to be having at the moment. When you get back to England, you must see a lawyer to get your son back."

"I will definitely do that," I promised, "but I must leave for the airport now."

He shouted for the police officer and told him to take me to the airport. Remanos shook my hand and wished me good luck. I smiled and we hugged like good friends do and I said goodbye. I had never been driven to the airport in a police car before and that in itself was an unusual experience. I can't imagine what people were thinking seeing me escorted to the airport by the police.

The lonely walk into a crowded airport was grim to say the least. I was returning home alone when I ought to have my family with me. I headed for the check-in desk and booked myself in. "Just one passenger?" the desk attendant asked with a smile.

"Yes," was all I could manage as the lump in my throat was threatening to choke me.

I walked through passport control wanting to be on the flight back to England as soon as possible. The flight home to England was the hardest thing I had ever done and the most emotional. I had flown out to Greece with a wife and child as a family. Next to me were two empty seats. I was a broken man with a broken heart. The plane took off and I glanced out of the window as we flew over Athens. My tears just started to flow. Somewhere down there were my wife and child. I silently said goodbye to Greece and promised myself that one day I would return. I shut my eyes all through the flight and I tried to get this nightmare out of my head. I can honestly say I had shed buckets of tears by the time I had landed in Manchester.

We touched down on time and as I was leaving the plane an air hostess touched my hand and asked if I were all right. It was pretty obvious I looked ill and possibly on a different planet. I just smiled with tears still rolling down my face. I walked through passport control totally oblivious of what was going on around me. I collected my suitcase and just walked away. In my grief, I even left behind a bag of birthday presents I had bought for Chris. I was too deep in thought to remember the gifts, but outside the airport my mum and step-dad, Jack, were waiting for me. As soon as she saw me, my mum rushed over and hugged me so tight I could have melted away in her arms. She had been rock and a shoulder to cry on. I said one word to her. "WHY?" She just looked and smiled as only a mother could.

The journey home was a short one, but a quiet one. I slept on my mum's shoulder all the way. I never spoke a word.

She took me to her house and I stayed there for a total of six weeks. I just couldn't face going into my own empty house, but as the days passed by, I grew stronger. My mum took me to a solicitor's office in Farnworth a couple of miles away. I told her everything and she reassured me that Christopher would be returned under The Hague Convention just like the embassy official had said. I signed all the paperwork and then she told me she was sending them off to the Lord Chancellor's Office in London. The department that deals with child abduction would represent me in my case. The solicitor told me it would take a while, but the Lord Chancellor's Office would get in touch with the abduction office in Greece and a date would be set for a court hearing for the safe return of Christopher.

Chapter 10 – Picking up the pieces.

The time had come when I had to go home and face my fears. I had to try to deal with the loss of Helen and Christopher. I considered it was like coping with a death in the family, but to me it was more frustrating. When a person dies, we all know we shall not see them again in this life, but Christopher was alive and well and these were human forces that seemed to be against me, not God's. I had to try to get my strength back somehow for the fight ahead and not allow those evil forces to grind me down.

After six weeks of staying with my mum, I felt a little better even though I had heard no news from Greece. It was Mum who decided it was time for me to go home.

"It's for the best, Ian," she said gently so as not to upset me. I looked at her with desperation in my eyes. "I don't think I'm ready yet, Mum. I really don't want to be in that house alone with all my memories. I don't think I can cope."

"You'll cope, love," she told me. "I know you will."

I knew Mum was right, so she and my step-dad took me home in their car. They dropped me off and let me go into the house on my own. I said goodbye and waved them off. Nervously I opened the door and just threw the suitcase down on the floor inside the door. I ran straight upstairs and went to bed even though it was only five in the evening. I couldn't bear to look at Christopher's room. I knew he wasn't in there and my heart sank at the thought of not seeing him. I felt so much pain inside when I thought about Christopher. I missed the simple things like holding him in my arms and reading bedtime stories and kissing goodnight and telling him how much I loved him. All of those things had been taken away from me by the person I had loved most in the world. It was certainly like grieving when somebody died. I knew Christopher was alive, but I had to try and get over the loss of him not being there with me and not being part of my life. The hardest thing for me was that I couldn't be a father to him and that felt like a dagger through my heart.

I was so scared of seeing all the memories of Christopher and Helen in the house. Running upstairs was my way of dealing with it. I didn't want to see the pictures of Helen and Christopher hanging on the walls. I walked into my bedroom and I could still smell Helen's perfume and see her nightdress on the bed where we had slept together. On my pillow was a teddy bear that Christopher had given to me. I sat on my bed with my head in my hands and wept.

Everywhere I looked, there were memories of Helen and Christopher. I felt could not bear the pain. I just wanted to die, to end my life, a life I could not face without Helen and my precious son. Had I had tablets in front of me at that moment, I would have taken the lot. I just got undressed and crawled into an empty bed. I cuddled Christopher's teddy bear and cried myself to sleep. I didn't want to wake up ever again. My life was not worth living without my family.

However, I did wake up the following morning still full of grief and despair. I went down the stairs and glanced at the pictures of Helen and Christopher on the wall. It broke my heart. In my desperation, I felt weak and ill. I sat on the couch and immediately felt sick. I ran upstairs and threw up. I felt so dizzy and I vomited for at least ten minutes. When I felt recovered enough to go downstairs again, I went into the kitchen where I could see Christopher's coat on the back of the chair. There was no escape. The reminders were everywhere I looked. In the back yard I saw the blue bike I had bought him for Christmas. His toys were all around the house. Hopelessness was devouring me and there was only one thing on my mind – death would be my only release from the agony I was suffering at that moment in time. I opened the kitchen drawer and picked up a box of painkillers. There must have been at least forty tablets inside. I sat at the table and looked at the box in my hand. I decided to write a short letter to my mother to tell her she was my rock and how much I loved her. I needed to thank her for always being there for me. I wrote a separate letter to Helen. My head was thumping and I could hardly open my eyes, but I carried on writing to Helen letting her know how much I loved her and how I couldn't understand why she left me. I told her I didn't regret anything in our life together and I always loved her. I asked her to tell Christopher that I loved him so much and it was the proudest day of my life when he was born. 'Ask him to forgive me for ending my life and one day when he gets older, I hope he will understand I could not face a life of pain, sadness and emptiness without him.'

I closed my eyes and prayed for forgiveness for taking my own life. Picking up the box of painkillers, I emptied them into my hand and put some in my mouth. Somehow, my throat seized up and I couldn't swallow them. Each time I tried, I vomited them back over the kitchen floor. It was that fortuitous physical rejection of the tablets that saved my life. Was it Fate? I don't know, but as the days passed by I gradually settled in the house again. It wasn't all plain sailing, but eventually, I was able to look at photographs again without getting upset. However, I didn't venture into Christopher's bedroom. I just could not face seeing all his toys and teddy bears, his things, his belongings. That was too much for me just then. It would be another two years before I could face going into his room.

One of the first things I needed to do was to go to Christopher's school and tell the headmaster what had happened. I made my way to St William of York Primary School and entered the school gates. When I saw Christopher's old classroom, I started to fill up. I couldn't help it, but I took a deep breath and pulled myself together. I went to see Mr Campbell, the headmaster. I sat in his office and told him what had happened in Greece. "I'm afraid Christopher will not be returning to school."

My eyes started to fill up again and my tears flowed, but after a moment, I pulled myself together yet again and thanked him for everything he had done for my son. I walked out through the school gates where I could see Christopher's friends. I turned away for the final time and walked down the back streets, not the route I used to take with Christopher on the way home from school. To go the usual way would have been too much for me to bear.

My aim now was to pick up the pieces and prepare for battle. I needed to be strong and I was determined to do everything in my power to win back my son. I would do it for the love of Christopher.

Chapter 11 – The power of my son's love.

I hadn't received any news about Christopher or Helen even though I had been in England for several weeks. I checked every morning to see if I had any letters from Helen, hoping that she had changed her mind and was coming home. Each day the postman would walk past my house and I would feel the pain when nothing was dropped through my door. As difficult as it was for me, I had to accept she was not going to come home with Christopher. My moods were up and down. It was an ongoing battle to cope with what was happening to me. The pain would not go away, not even with the medication prescribed by my doctor.

One day I decided to go to my mother's house. I needed her support. She was my rock who gave me the strength and love I needed to help me through the dark moments in my life.

She was glad to see me. I decided she needn't know about the attempt to end my life. I knew she would be very hurt and she didn't deserve that. If I had told her, she would have been extremely angry and I didn't want to upset her unnecessarily. I had cried so many times in front her and so many times she had held me in her arms and pulled me through.

On that particular day, she could see me hurting. Mothers have this uncanny sense of feeling their children's pain. With the tears about to roll down my cheeks again, she decided to make a phone call to Maria's house hoping to catch Helen. "I can but try," she told me. "Surely she will have some mercy and allow me to speak to Christopher."

I was hoping and praying that my mum would speak to Christopher so I could hear his voice. Maria answered the phone. "Hello?"

"Maria, this is Ian's mother. Please may I speak to Helen?" my mother asked in her most polite voice.

Almost immediately Helen was on the phone. "Hello?"

My mum was careful what she said. "Hello Helen. Do you think I might speak to Christopher?"

I was very surprised when there was no argument and at least it confirmed that Helen was staying at her mother's house. Mum held the phone near my ear so I could hear Christopher's voice.

"Hello?" came the little voice from Greece.

I grabbed the phone from my mum and spoke to Christopher. "Hi, Christopher," I said quietly.

"Dad?" he asked.

"I'm here," I told him, "and I love and miss you very much."

I heard Christopher catch his breath and he replied in a tearful voice that will haunt me for the rest of my life. "My mum won't let me come home."

Suddenly the phone was cut off. I was so angry. I could feel the rage rising from deep inside and that was the defining moment that changed my whole attitude to life. I felt so ashamed that I tried to kill myself. It was the harsh realisation of what it would have done to Christopher had I ended my life. It would have destroyed him and I knew from the way he spoke on the phone that he still loved me. Hearing his voice empowered me.

I promised myself to be strong for my family and for me. I had to carry on the fight and get my revenge. If it meant punishing Helen's family for what they had done, then so be it. I hugged my mother. "I don't know what I would do without you," I told her. "You are always there for me and I love you for it more than you will ever know."

"I do know, Ian," she told me. "You are my son and I'd go to the ends of the earth for you."

I returned home knowing I was confident and I was ready for the fight. At the beginning of November 1998, I received a letter from the abduction department in London informing me of the date for a court hearing in Athens to bring Christopher home.

Chapter 12 – A court hearing at last – or was it?

The first person I called when I received the letter from the Lord Chancellor's Office in London, was my mum.

"I've got a date," I told her excitedly.

"A date?" she asked confused.

"A date for the hearing," I explained with a smile on my face.

"Jack and I will come with you," she said. "We'll be your star witnesses."

We were both very excited at the prospects of bringing Christopher home to the land of his birth, to his friends at school and to everything he knew so well. I wasn't sure what the Greek courts were like, but I knew we had the law on our side as far as the abduction was concerned. I had three weeks to prepare myself and I needed to book the flights and the hotel for my mum, Jack and me. For the first time since Christopher had been abducted by his mother, Helen, I had hope in my heart. Gone were the dark days when I finally went back to my home in Alder Street and attempted to end my life. Optimism had taken over and I felt strong enough to face anything Helen threw at me in court.

My new-found good humour encouraged me to go out for a drink on a Saturday night with friends. I couldn't stop smiling and telling everybody that Christopher would be coming home soon. I wanted everybody to know how optimistic I was about going to Greece in a couple of weeks and bringing Christopher home with me at last. The night before we were flying out, I stayed at my mother's so we could travel together to Manchester airport. We had a few beers and felt confident we would be bringing Christopher back with us. Under The Hague Convention, the child must be returned to his country of residence where the courts of that country would make a decision on the future of the child.

We had an early night so as to be up bright and early for the six o'clock flight. I was happy at the prospect of Christopher coming home. I slept well for the first time in ages.

With all the check-in procedures over, we were finally on our flight, eager and hopeful of a wonderful outcome to our trip. Christopher was foremost in our thoughts and when we arrived in Athens, we took a taxi to Omonia Square and our hotel. Omonia Square is in downtown Athens, an old area in the north of the city with good roads out and served by the Omonia train station. It wasn't a very pleasant place to stay, but convenient and with good connections to Piraeus where the court was situated. We had a few days in Athens until the court case, so I took the opportunity to show my mother and Jack around my favourite sites, especially the Acropolis and other historical locations.

We went to a few bars, had a few drinks and we were pretty relaxed. Personally, I was just happy to be there in Greece. I was really looking forward to wiping the smile of Helen's and her parents' faces. The night before the court case, we visited the Alexandra bar where I used to go with Helen. Greek music was playing in the background while we were drinking the local beer. When in Greece, do as the

Greeks do! We all seemed to be relaxed and having a great time. Afterwards, we went for a walk round Tourkolimano. It is a port in Piraeus and has a beautiful harbour with ships from all over the world. There are bars and plenty of restaurants with all different cuisines. It's more expensive for drinks and food as it's a millionaire's paradise, but when walking along the harbour, the aroma of local dishes like fish and chicken and all kinds of meats is very appetising. At night, the harbour is lit up and is very picturesque. It's a beautiful place to visit and just what we needed the night before the court hearing.

While my mum and Jack were chatting, I allowed my mind to drift back to the times when Helen, Christopher and I used to go for walks around there, but I had to be ready and alert in court the next day. Dwelling on those times wouldn't help. The showdown with Helen and her family was looming.

We got up early and had breakfast. I looked at Mum and she seemed relaxed and chirpy and Jack was very chatty and full of his usual humour. He was telling his corny jokes I had heard many times before, but I knew he was trying to keep our spirits high and stop us worrying about the hearing. Nothing ever fazed him. He was as tough as they come. We made our way to the Metro, caught a train to Piraeus and then a taxi to the Greek Court of First Instance on Skouze Street. We dressed smartly to create a good impression.

My Greek lawyer met us and she told us the court case had to be adjourned, because Helen hadn't turned up. "What happens now?" I asked. I was furious that we had travelled from England and the hearing could be adjourned, just like that, because of Helen's stupidity.

"The hearing will be set for another date," my lawyer informed us, "probably for some time in December. It is only a few weeks away."

I sighed. "I could accept that if I hadn't had to fly in from England," I told her. "I know Helen. She'll be hoping we'll run out of money and the case will be dropped."

"I agree," the lawyer said, "but Helen can't do this again. If she does, she will be in serious trouble."

Disappointed didn't come close to how I felt and Mum and Jack were just as dejected as I was. I had been so convinced I would be taking Christopher home and those dreams had been dashed in a matter of seconds. We left the court feeling totally let down and we thought if we went for something to eat, it would make us feel better. Kentucky fried chicken did the trick!

Jack loved Kentucky fried chicken, in fact, that's all he lived on while we were in Greece. In truth, I was so frustrated that I just wasn't in the mood to eat anything. I looked at my mum and I knew she was unhappy, but she put on a brave face as usual, for my benefit, I'm sure.

We decided to go to Helen's house to try to see Christopher. We were all determined that our trip to Greece wouldn't be wasted. I wasn't afraid of facing the family, especially with my mum and Jack behind me. I felt much safer than I had the last time. As we walked up the hill to the house, we passed the bar where I first met Helen in 1990. I tried not to let my mind go over those times again. The hill up to the house was long and steep and Mum and Jack really struggled. They were both in their seventies and it seemed to take us forever. Each time we stopped so they could rest, I couldn't help but hark back to the past and the number of times I had climbed that hill. There were good times and bad and although I didn't want to dwell on the past, it was inevitable that every step I took towards the house would bring back memories, the worst one being when Christopher had been stolen out of my life.

When the house came into view, I saw Christopher on the balcony. "Christopher!" I called out as I waved to him. I was so happy to see him. Christopher just stood and looked at us. I could see him smiling at me, but Maria then took his arm and pulled him inside. My stomach was turning inside-out as we climbed the steps to her front door, the same door and stairs down which she had thrown my suitcase. The door opened before we had time to knock and Maria stood there glaring at us. I did not smile or speak to her, but just pushed past her and went in. Helen was standing just inside with Christopher and Vangelis. I didn't look at Helen or Vangelis. I did not smile or speak to her. Why should I? I picked Christopher up and held in my arms. I didn't cry or show any emotion. I was determined to be strong for Christopher who was so happy to see me. He told me to wait one minute and he went off into his bedroom. He was gone a few minutes and during that time I dared to look at Helen. She showed no emotion. Her expression was blank and I guessed she didn't know how to deal with the situation.

The atmosphere in the house was very creepy because Maria and Vangelis didn't speak one word while we were there. Mum and Jack didn't seem to be perturbed at all so I felt very safe with them there with me. Christopher returned and gave me a drawing. When I looked at it and saw what he had written - I love my daddy – it brought my first smile to my face since I had arrived in Maria's house. We weren't there more than twenty minutes. I simply focused my attention on Christopher. I wanted to enjoy every minute with him, because I didn't know when I would see him again.

When it was time to leave, my mum held Christopher in her arms. She didn't show any emotion, but she kissed him and told him she loved him. Jack took hold of Christopher's hand and said, "See you soon," as he kissed him on his cheek.

I gave Christopher a hug and kissed him goodbye. "I love you very much. Always remember that. I'll see you soon." I smiled just for him as we left the house. All three of us walked out without saying a word or making any kind of eye contact with Helen, or her parents. We owed them nothing.

As we walked down the hill, I turned round just once to see if Christopher was on the balcony, but he was nowhere to be seen. That was the only time I saw Christopher in all the time I was there. I was so proud of myself for not showing my feelings in front of Helen and her parents. My mum and Jack kept their thoughts to themselves and I was glad about that. I appreciated that they were allowing me to deal with the situation in my own way. Discussing it would only bring back the old heartache and I didn't want that.

SEVEN-YEAR-OLD SEIZED BY HIS MOTHER'S FAMILY IN GREECE

Battling evil of abduction

The last two days before we went home, my mum and Jack wanted to go round the shops. I was happy to give them space and I did my own thing. I went round the local bars in Omonia Square drinking ouzo and reflecting on the day's events. I had seen Christopher and that made me happy. It made up for the frustration of the hearing being adjourned, but I lived to fight another day. Next time I came to Greece, I would be taking my son home with me. We flew back to England and even though it had been a big disappointment, I was more than made up by seeing Christopher, hearing him say he loved me and the note he had given me. All those things gave me hope that one day we would be together again. Mum, Jack and I had a drink of wine on the plane and agreed the battle may be lost, but we would return with renewed enthusiasm to win the war.

Chapter 13 – Feminine wiles?

The court case was looming and I didn't know what to expect. I didn't trust Helen and her family and I hadn't a clue whether or not they were going to turn up in court. I had already booked my flight along with my mum and step-dad, Jack. The night before the flight, I decided to go out on the town for a few beers. There had been a lot of publicity about Christopher's abduction and no matter where I went, people, male and female, were coming up to me, asking what was happening with my son. What was intended to be a quiet drink turned out to be 'question time' at the bar. I appreciated their interest, but I didn't want to talk about the court case just before I was due to fly out to Greece, so decided to go back home. I didn't sleep much that night. I was thinking about Christopher and wondering if Helen would turn up.

I was up very early in order to be at Manchester airport for the morning flight. I had ordered a taxi to leave from my mother's house. We were all going in the same taxi to the airport. It seemed the most sensible. It was Saturday morning and we were going to stay in Athens for a week. I knew the court case was for real and the battling would begin.

We stayed in the same hotel as before in Omonia Square. We had three days to chill out before the court case on the Tuesday and I was adamant I would relax as much as possible.

The first two days, my mum and Jack visited the shops as usual, the clothes shops and lots of the souvenir shops. I visited the Acropolis as I always did whenever I visited Greece. I had always been fascinated by Greek history. I would just stare at the Acropolis shining like a lit-up wedding cake above the city. It felt like a magnet drawing me to it. That icon of ancient Athens was real to me now, no longer just a picture on a postcard or an image in a guide book. It was much better than seeing it in a movie and I felt inspired by it. Each view presented me with a photo opportunity and my camera was always at the ready.

While my mum was unpacking, I sneaked out and rang Helen to ask if it were all right to see Christopher. Much to my surprise, she agreed and told me to go on the Monday as they would be busy till then. On Saturday and Sunday, it was chill out time for us all. We went to a few bars and we had a good laugh and joked around. We were totally relaxed and we didn't mention the court case that was happening on Tuesday. On the Monday, I made the excuse I was going to Piraeus for a while. I didn't want to tell Mum and Jack I was seeing Helen and Christopher. I knew they would persuade me not to go, but I just had to see my little boy before the hearing. I had the confidence to go on my own knowing neither Helen, Maria, nor Vangelis would risk doing anything stupid with the court case the following day.

On my way there, I called at the police station in Perama to see if Remanos was on duty. He was sitting at the front desk with his feet up watching television. I laughed to myself thinking things would never change there with Remanos in charge. We gave each other a hug. He was happy to see me and he pulled a bottle of vodka out of his drawer as he winked and smiled at me with his broad infectious smile. I told him what was going on, about the court case and everything. I stayed about twenty minutes and told him I was going to Helen's house to see Christopher.

"Be careful, Ian," he said. "You and I know what they are like. Shall I take you up there to make sure you are all right?"

"Thanks, Remanos, but I'll be fine," I told him. "They won't dare try anything today just before the hearing." I said my goodbyes and left him.

As usual I walked up the long hill to Helen's house. I had nicknamed it the hill of tears after all the bad experiences I had had. I walked past the cafe bar where Helen and I used to go for a drink and a meal. It was the place where I'd hid in disguise on that fateful day when I surprised her and planned her escape out of Greece. I passed the small park where Christopher used to play. It was impossible not to recall all these things as I walked past all the familiar places.

When I arrived at the house, I stopped, took a deep breath and made my way up the stairs. Helen was waiting for me at the top. She smiled and let me in. Vangelis wasn't there and Maria was in her bedroom which seemed strange to me. Helen took me onto the balcony as it was a lovely day for sitting outside. She was very chirpy and went out of her way to be nice to me. I found it all very odd and decided it was because she was going to lose the court case and was trying to befriend me again. She was asking questions about Alder Street where we had lived together and about my family and friends. It was bizarre considering we were all in court the following day.

Ian and Christopher in Greece

Christopher came on the balcony and sat on my knee. He was very talkative and loving and it made me very happy. It confirmed he still loved me. I played with him for over an hour, something I had missed very much; one of the simple things of being a father. We played Snap, a card game we always played in England. I stayed a while longer and Helen asked me where I was staying. I told her the name of the hotel and where it was situated. I actually felt quite comfortable, but the time came for me to leave. "I must go," I told her.

"Oh, can't you stay longer?" she asked.

"No, I must get back to my mum and Jack. They will be wondering where I am." As I was leaving, she shook my hand and said goodbye. I gave Christopher a big hug and kissed him. "See you later, Chris."

As I was walking down the hill Helen shouted at me and waved. I don't know why I did it, but I waved back at her. I was letting my guard down and it was a dangerous thing to do when the next day we would be enemies in court.

When I arrived back at the hotel, the receptionist told me there was a message for me. It was from Helen. I looked at it wide-eyed. 'Meet me at the train station at 9pm.'

I felt totally confused. I didn't understand what was going on and what her intentions were. I met my mother and Jack and we went for a meal in a small cafe in Omonia Square. Jack wanted to go to KFC, his usual haunt, but my mum put her foot down and we went elsewhere. We had Greek food - Souvlaki which was like a small kebab with salad and chips. I told them I was going out later, but I made the excuse I was touring a few bars. I told Mum and Jack I needed to chill with the up-coming court case the following day. I didn't tell them I was meeting Helen as I knew they would be very annoyed.

I had already dressed for dinner so after we had our meal, I left Mum and Jack. "I'll see you later," I said. "I won't be late in."

Mum was worried. "Be careful," she pleaded. "I don't like the thought of you being out on your own at night."

"I'll be okay, Mum," I reassured her. "Don't worry."

I got a taxi to Piraeus wondering what the hell Helen wanted with me. I didn't understand it at all. I arrived early, but Helen was already there. She was dressed as though she was going on a date. Alarm bells should have been ringing. She was wearing a white see-through blouse displaying her ample breasts for all to see, black pants and white strappy shoes. Her long blonde hair fell in curls onto her shoulders; her luscious lips were shiny with pink lipstick and her green eyes were gleaming in the moonlight. She looked so beautiful and it took all my powers of restraint not to tell her.

"Why do you want to see me?" I asked.

"Let's go to the Alexander bar where we can talk," she replied. She smiled. "It's where we used to go, remember?"

"How could I forget?" I answered, still confused.

It seemed that the whole population of Athens was in that bar, but I ordered a bottle of retsina. We both liked the exclusive Greek wine with its pungent taste; although it is not to everybody's liking. The waiter came over and started to play a violin near our table. It was very romantic. The sense of the occasion started to affect me. The court case was forced to the back of my mind. I ought to have been more aware of what was happening, but the drinks were flowing and Helen was getting closer to me by the minute. Neither of us mentioned the hearing and as the night wore on, I didn't care.

I was very comfortable around Helen. I was totally bewitched by her. I gazed into her eyes and all the feelings I had for her came back. I could see the old Helen and I couldn't keep my eyes off her beautiful face and her voluptuous body. I touched her hand pulling her close enough to kiss her. When our lips met, I was lost. I was still in love with her; my feelings just came flooding back and I couldn't think about the bad things that had happened between us.

A young gypsy girl came over. She was only a child, but she placed a red rose on the table. I gave the child a hundred drachmas and I gave the rose to Helen. She bent over and gave me a long lingering kiss. I was falling in love with her again and I didn't try to stop myself. I was totally overwhelmed with passion.

The night was becoming more and more romantic. We couldn't stop touching each other. Catching my breath, I asked her, "Would you like to go to a hotel?"

"Yes," she breathed huskily and it completely made my raging passion take over.

We jumped into a taxi and went to the same hotel where I stayed when I smuggled her out of Greece. Once in the room, we stripped off, delighting in our nakedness and we made love over and over again; love or lust? In hindsight, I don't know, but it was just like the old times if not better.

"I love you so much, Ian," she whispered. "I realised how much I have missed you when you came to the house this afternoon."

"I love you too," I told her. "I always did."

I didn't care if she was enticing me into a web of deceit. I just wanted to be with her. I was so happy that she loved me. I cried in her arms and I didn't want that moment to end. When I looked into her eyes, she was crying too.

She held me close and said, "You will hate me for what I'm going to say tomorrow in the court." She didn't elaborate on what she meant.

Maybe I ought to have insisted she told me the details, but I just told her I loved her and I just wanted to cherish that moment. We got dressed and left the hotel. We kissed again and that was it. She left in a taxi.

I made my way back to the hotel in the early hours of the morning. I went straight to bed happy, with a big smile on my face completely unaware of what would happen in court the following day. For then, I went to sleep a happy man.

Chapter 14 – My love; her lies.

The day of the second hearing had arrived. Mum, Jack and I got up early for our breakfast. This was no ordinary breakfast. We made it a pre-victory meal. I chose not to mention anything about the eventful evening I had had with

Helen. I was sure Mum and Jack would have been shocked and angry thinking I might have jeopardised the hearing. Even then there was a bit of tension in the air. We needed to relax and be ready for our appearance in court. Part of my preparation was to look at a small picture of Christopher I kept in my pocket; looking at him gave me strength to cope.

Looking at my mother, I could see for the first time the nervousness behind her smile. Jack was the same as ever. Nothing seemed to bother him, which was good for Mum and me. We knew we could always depend on him in the event of any trouble. We didn't go to the court by train this time. We went by taxi straight to the Court of the First Instance. We arrived there bright and early and I felt fine. After my night out with Helen, I wasn't nervous at all.

I was waiting near the doorway when I saw Helen coming in with her mum and Christopher. I looked around to see Vangelis outside talking to four taxi drivers. When Vangelis walked past Jack, he passed a comment. He spoke in Greek so Jack didn't know what he said, but he could tell by the tone of Vangelis' voice that it wasn't complimentary. Undeterred, Jack looked him in the eye. "Bastard," he spat in the same tone as Vangelis. "Let the battle begin."

I was going to face up to Vangelis and tell him to watch his step, but my mum grabbed me and said, "Not in here, Ian. He's trying to provoke you into a fight and make you look bad in court."

I knew she was right and in actual fact, Vangelis had done me a favour, because he'd fired me up in preparation for the fray. I was ready for the fight. Bring it on!

When my lawyer arrived she came straight over. She was gabbling a bit and she seemed very nervous. I asked her what time we were due in court and she said, "Very soon."

"Will we be able to take Christopher home straight away?" I asked hoping there would be no delay after the hearing.

"The judge might decide that the child should be with his mother," she warned us.

I wasn't pleased with her answer. In fact I was horrified and my anger flared. "You fight for me, not for Helen and you're wrong. You must go by European law." I was beginning to doubt my lawyer and wonder if she was fully trained. She was only about twenty-four years old and she was starting to annoy me. I told her in no uncertain terms that under The Hague Convention, it was up to the courts in the country of the child's residence to decide what is best for that child.

"The child should be with his mother," she said bluntly.

Eventually we went inside the courtroom. "It's time," my lawyer told us, but I couldn't believe what I was seeing. There were people in a line in front of the judge who had his say then pressed a bell for the next one in line to be dealt with. It was farcical. It looked like queuing up at the check-out in a supermarket. The court room wasn't big, but it was packed to the rafters with offenders, their families and their lawyers. It was total chaos. I was standing next to petty criminals and I asked my Greek lawyer to try to explain to me what was going on.

"I thought this was to be a private hearing," I told her. To my disgust, she just shrugged her shoulders.

We were forced to watch the proceedings before us. Each offender had his own lawyer in front of the judge and there would be a bit of shouting and waving of arms until the judge gave his verdict. When he rang his bell, the next in line was dealt with. Talk about a comedy show.

When they were all finished, the courtroom emptied and we were told by our lawyer to sit down. It was then Helen, Vangelis and Maria came in and sat down along with their lawyer. I couldn't see Christopher and I was wondering where he was. I looked at Helen who seemed very tired. She glanced at me, but she didn't smile. Both our lawyers were laughing and joking together. I thought, *what the hell is going on here?* You can't be friends with the opposing lawyer for Christ sake! And to make matters worse, my lawyer came over to me to tell me the translator couldn't make it.

I started to go blue in the face. I was beginning to think, *this is a bloody set up.* In the end, they had to get some bloke out of an office who could speak only very basic English to translate for the judge. I looked at him and thought, *this is a piss take.* His English is no better than my Greek. However, the proceedings got underway and you could hear a pin drop, not at all like the court cases that had gone before ours with all the arguing and shouting. This is where the battling begins, I thought, but it turned out to be so full of dramatic dishonesty; a one sided fight that I couldn't control.

Vangelis was the first one up. The lies and the venom that came out of his mouth were unreal. He said things which shocked and amazed me. He told the judge Helen and I had never had any money and that he had to support us over the years by paying our bills and he had to send food parcels to England. He also said he had visited us in England and we had no furniture in the house. He told the court I was abusive to my wife and child, I was gay and had a drink problem. According to him, Helen had been unhappy from the first day we were together. They were all lies and everybody except the judge knew it.

The truth was, he never once came to England. Only Maria came when Helen and I went to Paris. The judge was writing down all his lies. I told my lawyer he was lying and asked her, "Why don't you stand up for me?" The hatred I had formed for Vangelis would stay with me forever. My lawyer looked at me and said nothing. I couldn't believe it. I thought it would be just a case of going in front of the judge and under The Hague Convention, Christopher would be coming back home to England with me.

After he had finished, Vangelis walked past me, winked and smiled evilly. The look I gave him was one of pure hatred, but it was now my mother's turn to speak. I was astounded that the judge treated her like a criminal when he questioned her. She was in her seventies at the time and the most caring and loving mother anybody could ever have. "Is your son gay?" he asked. "Is he an alcoholic and has he ever been abusive towards his wife and child?"

My mother was in tears and told the judge it was all lies. She tried her best, but it was Helen's lawyer's turn to ask the questions and the false accusations just kept coming out of his mouth. My lawyer did nothing to stop this and my mother was so overcome by it all, her spirit was broken. The whole situation was becoming one big drama that should not be happening in a court of law. She had gone all that way to support me and now she was devastated by the way she was being treated. My heart sank and I couldn't hide the sadness in my eyes. I felt so vulnerable. There was my mother who was my rock, a woman who had stood by all her children over the years even though she had suffered at the hands of my father and I had to sit and watch her being torn apart. The treatment she received scared her and I know it will affect her for the rest of her life. I was so angry. I loved my mother very much. She had her head in her arms and I felt desperately sorry for her.

Next, it was my turn and Helen's to face the judge and both lawyers. Helen was standing next to me, very quiet and very nervous. I knew I had to face the wrath from Helen's lawyer and he told the judge the same lies Vangelis had told them. He then produced a drawing which I was supposed to have done myself. He looked at me with pure anger. The drawing was of a Greek man with his head having been cut off with a knife.

"Did you draw this?" he asked.

"No, I did not," I stated firmly.

Helen's lawyer was trying to convince the court that I hated Greek people. My translator was useless. He couldn't speak much English and my lawyer didn't do much to help me. It was looking so one-sided and I thought I was definitely being set up.

The judge asked Helen the same questions and she agreed with everything Vangelis and her lawyer had said. As for me, I said I still loved my wife and my child and that drawing was certainly not done by me. Standing beside me was the girl I loved so much and the night before we had made love all night. I remembered the words she had said me - you will hate me with what I'm going to say in court. It just never sank in. I could never have imagined the seriousness of the situation she would put me in. To say that I was hurt and humiliated comes nowhere near how I felt.

I was told to sit down. Helen did not look at me once. I was devastated. I thought she loved me and yet she allowed me to be humiliated in court and allowed her lawyer to destroy my mother who had accepted Helen into our family and loved her like a daughter. I looked at my mother and she looked at me with total sadness in her eyes. The anger drained from me. I was a broken man.

The court proceedings stopped and I was told by my lawyer that the judge wanted to see Helen and me on our own to see if we could patch things up. We sat in a small room with the judge. "Do you want to go home?" he asked Helen.

She said, "No."

He asked her again. "Do you love your husband?"

She said, "No."

He then asked me, "Do you love her?"

I said, "Yes and I love my son too."

He asked her for the final time, "Do you want to go to England?"

She said, "No."

I had been completely deceived by the girl I met in Corfu and with whom I went through so much to take her to England; who was the mother of my child and who had despicably allowed my mother and me be destroyed in court.

It was the end of the meeting. Helen walked out. I waited a few minutes before I left. My mum and Jack were waiting for me at the entrance. It was then I saw Helen with Christopher and Maria. Vangelis was with same Greek guys he had been talking to before the hearing. They were obviously there for a purpose - to protect him and to stop me grabbing Christopher. I wanted to kill Vangelis after what he had done to my family. He smirked at me and drove away with Helen, Chris and Maria who I truly hated at that time and still do to this day.

Outside the court, I held my mother in my arms and I told her I was sorry for putting her through the ordeal. We went back to the hotel and my mum was very quiet and deep in thought. She went in to her room and slept for the rest of the day. The only way I could try to forget the events of the day, was to go for a drink. I had to face it; I was betrayed by the woman I truly loved and I drowned my sorrows by drinking ouzo to blank out my pain.

Chapter 15 – Heart rules head.

I didn't sleep much after the hearing. My mother and Jack seemed to be two different people after Mum's ordeal in court. The last couple of days of our time in Greece were sad affairs. We didn't discuss the court case. Maybe we should have, but the pain was still deep and I don't think any of us wanted to live through it again. My mother looked ill. She was very pale and her eyes looked very tired. She was a shell of her former self and I felt guilty that I had subjected her to all this.

On the morning we were flying back, I received a phone call in my room. It was Helen and she wanted to meet me outside the Metro station. I really don't know why I even considered it. I was feeling depressed and I was still very angry with her.

"Please, Ian, please meet me," she begged. "I have to explain all those things I said in court."

I don't know why I agreed to meet her, but I did. I certainly wanted to find out why Helen had tried to destroy me in court. I went to see my mother and I lied to her again. "I need to clear my head," I said, and tried not to look guilty."I'm going for a walk around the city. I want to leave all my memories behind, and leave them where they were made if you see what I mean."

Mum nodded her head. I knew she was weary of it all and so she simply let me get on with what I said I had to do. "Okay." Jack didn't say anything. I didn't know what he was thinking, but I knew he was still upset by the way they had treated my mum in court.

I caught the train to Piraeus which didn't take long - about thirty minutes in all. My emotions were playing tricks me. I had butterflies in my stomach. I didn't want to be excited about seeing Helen after what she did to my mum and me in court. In spite of all that, I travelled to meet her even though I felt I betrayed my mum in doing so. I shouldn't have been anywhere near Helen, but I was following my heart for the most basic of all reasons – love.

Helen was already there when I arrived and I noted she wasn't dressed like the night I stayed out with her. She was dressed in jeans and tee-shirt. It crossed my mind that her seductive clothing had worked the night before the hearing, but she obviously wasn't there to seduce me again. She wasn't shy at all with me. She just came straight out with it and said, "I'm sorry." I looked at her in disgust. "Can we go for a coffee so we can talk?" she asked.

I stared at her with wide angry eyes. "I'm not going anywhere with you. You have a cheek asking to see me after what you did. I don't think I could ever forgive you."

"Please, Ian," she begged. "Please come for a coffee so I can explain."

We went into a cafe in a side street. It was only small, nothing special, but I didn't care. "I can't believe I'm even here speaking to you, let alone having a coffee with you. Just get on with it; the sooner this is over, the better then I can go back to the hotel."

I bought her a coffee and I had a beer. She told me it was her lawyer who made her and her family say those things about me in court. "He told me I had no choice if I wanted to keep Christopher. I didn't want to lose him forever."

I just looked at her, dumbfounded. I was numb inside. Didn't she realise that was exactly how I was feeling? I didn't want to lose Christopher forever either. Those feelings weren't solely reserved for her. She had lied in court to keep Christopher and all I did was tell the truth. We both had a right as parents to keep him, but in this sad case, I had the law on my side as far as the Hague Convention was concerned. Christopher had been born in England, was English and English courts had to decide his future. She was crying and asking for forgiveness. She held my hand and begged me.

"All I said in court was that I loved you," I reminded her. "Even after all the bad things you said against me. We had made love the night before and you said you loved me. What am I supposed to do, Helen?"

She was crying bitterly. "I'm sorry. I still love you. I want you to stay in Greece with Christopher and me. We can both get jobs and our own house and live a happy life together."

I gasped at what she was saying. "What?' I questioned. "Vangelis and Maria hate me. I couldn't live under their scrutiny all the time."

"They have both agreed that you can stay in their house until we can find our own place to live," she told me.

My head was all over the place. I couldn't forgive her, but deep down I still loved her and wanted to be with her and Christopher more than anything else in the world. I was numb and so tired and still crying inside. She had confused me more than ever, but I kissed her goodbye thinking it I would be forever.

When I arrived back at the hotel, my mum was waiting for me and she wasn't pleased. "Where have you been? You are the late and we have to go to the airport now," she snapped. Jack had already brought my suitcase down to reception. I knew they were annoyed with me, but I didn't say anything about where I had been.

Just as we were leaving the hotel, the telephone rang at the reception desk and the receptionist called out that the call was for me. It was Helen begging me again to go to the house. She was crying and sounded desperate.

"I can't," I said bluntly and then put the phone down.

"Who was that?" my mother asked.

"Nobody important," I said. "Come on, let's get going."

During the taxi ride to the airport, we were all quiet. I was thinking about Helen and Christopher and how I wanted to be with them. How on earth could I tell my mother and Jack that I wanted to stay in Greece? I knew it would break my mother's heart and Jack would be very angry with me. I struggled with my conscience, but I had to do what I felt was right for Christopher and for me.

We arrived at the airport and I still couldn't keep Helen out of my mind. We checked in and made our way to Passport Control. My mind was racing. *What the hell am I going to do? I have to make a decision and quick!*

My mother and Jack walked through the barriers. I stopped dead. My mother stopped and turned round. "Come on, Ian. We have to go."

I just looked at her and fought back my tears. "I'm sorry, Mum. I can't come home with you. My life has to be in Greece now."

I could see my poor mother breaking up. She had gone all that way to defend me in court. I had been devastated by the treatment she had received and now I was expecting her to understand what I was doing for my own reasons. "Bye, both of you. I'm sorry. I love you." I didn't know what else I could say.

As I walked away, I turned round and saw Jack holding my mother in his arms. I knew my mother would be heart-broken. I was upset by what I was doing to them, but I loved my wife and child and I simply could not leave them behind in Greece. I felt my place was with my wife and child in Greece. I hoped my mother and Jack would understand why I couldn't leave my family and live alone in England. My suitcase had to be taken off the plane and after I collected it, I headed for the exit. I watched with tears in my eyes as the plane took off carrying my mum and Jack back to England. It weighed heavily on my conscience, but my heart strings were pulling me in another direction.

All the way to Helen's house, I couldn't stop thinking about my mum and Jack and I had to wonder if I were doing the right thing. Surprisingly, Maria was smiling when she met me at the door. Vangelis was on his way out, but he shook my hand as he left. Christopher was playing with his toys and was happy to see me. "Come and play with me, Dad," he said as I went in. I played with him for a while just like the old days. I had longed for that dad and lad situation and for it to happen again was magical for me.

Helen acted as though nothing had happened. She was very chatty and loving towards me and the first thing she asked was, "Are you going to drop the kidnapping charges now?"

"In the morning," I said without enthusiasm. "Let's not think about that just now."

She led me onto the balcony with Christopher. She seemed so happy and kissed me occasionally to show affection. We were on the balcony for a while talking about our new life in Greece and what the future held for us. There was something about the way Helen described what our lives would be like that made me silently question my decision. The more we talked, the less I was sure about living in Greece. I kept looking at Helen and thinking to myself, I can't trust her even though I love her. How can I possibly live in this house where Maria tried to break up our relationship when I first came to Athens? Doubts were creeping into my mind. I gazed around the house trying to find something to convince me to stay, but there was nothing. I hated Maria and Vangelis with a passion and I could never forgive them for what they had done. Helen had been very quick to ask me to drop the kidnapping charges. 'Are you going to drop the kidnapping charges now?' Did Helen's question hold the key to why they were so keen to have me back in their home? Would they kick me out again once I had dropped the charges? I wanted Christopher to go back home to England, the land of his birth. I wanted the right to take him there, but not at the price they were charging. I realised I had made a very big mistake in returning to their house.

That night, when we went to bed, we made love and clung together, enjoying the closeness of our bodies and the gentleness of each other's touch. As Helen slept, I held her close for the final time and whispered in her ear, "I love you, my Greek princess and I always will. I kissed her on the cheek and turned over. Sleep evaded me. Thoughts of Mum and Jack played on my mind. I needed to be in my home in England, not in the home of people I did not trust. I knew I loved Helen, but that was simply not enough. Eventually, I went to sleep knowing I would carry on the fight take Christopher home where he belonged.

In the morning, Helen was really happy especially as she thought I was going to drop the kidnapping charges. I knew she would be afraid of going to prison and that's why she had come on strongly to me the night before. We left the house and walked down the hill, the hill that had featured so many times in my life during the past year. There would be no more weeping as this would be the final time we walked together down that hill of tears. When we arrived at the bus station, I silently confirmed I would be going home to carry on the fight for Christopher to finally take him home.

I stopped and turned to Helen. "I'm not staying in Greece," I told her clearly. "It's not what I want and it's not what I want for Christopher."

I could see her temper rising. "What?" she yelled. "You rotten English bastard! You led me on to think you would stay."

"No, you led me on," I said with very little feeling and I walked away to go back to the house for my suitcase. I said nothing to Maria, but when Christopher saw me with my luggage, he began to cry.

"Why are you leaving, Dad?" he asked plaintively.

I held him in my arms and I kissed him affectionately. "I'll see you soon. Don't worry. I love you very much and I always will. I promise I won't forget you and please don't forget me." Tears were rolling down my face, but I smiled at Christopher and I walked away, out of Helen's life forever.

On the way down the hill, I smiled as I thought I would never see this hill again. I was so happy about that and would I miss it? Not one little bit!

I booked a flight home to England and phoned my mother to tell her I was going home. I wasn't sure how she would react, but when I heard her voice, I knew she was relieved. "I'm happy about that," she told me. "I'll be glad when you are home."

I was full of guilt when I said, "I'm sorry about the way I treated you and Jack, Mum. I thought I needed to give Christopher the chance of having me around while he was growing up. I soon realised it was Helen's way of getting me to drop the charges. I don't think she, Maria, or Vangelis had any other reason to have me under their roof. I'm so sorry I hurt you."

"I understand now, love," she told me, "but I was shocked when you didn't get on that plane with us; all in the past now, eh? Just be careful and come home safely."

At the risk of repeating myself, I cannot emphasise enough that my mother was my rock. I loved and admired her more than words could ever say. She had so much strength and love to give and she carried me through all the bad times. She was one very special lady in my life.

For once, I was happy when I arrived at the airport. I felt strong and not at odds with the world as I had previously. I had walked out of Helen's life forever and I was determined to have Christopher home soon - just the two us. I looked down from the plane onto the Greek landscape. I smiled and told myself, "I will not be coming back." Soon Christopher would be home with me. I was happy for the first time in ages.

Chapter 16 – Living with my loss.

The flight home seemed to be longer than usual. I was happy with myself that I had left Helen the way I did. I had wanted to give Helen a taste of her own medicine. Revenge is sweet and I certainly felt justified in what I had done. I walked out of her life forever and all I needed at that point was the court's decision about Christopher.

The first thing I did was to visit my mother and Jack to see if they were all right. They were glad to see me and Jack wasn't angry with me. I apologised again for everything they had gone through in Greece, particularly when I didn't return home with them.

"We understand," Jack said, "but we were concerned about your safety, Ian. Your deciding to stay wasn't the issue.

Knowing that you might not be safe with Helen's family was our biggest problem."

We talked all day about the events in Greece and I could see my mum was still deeply upset although she tried her best to conceal it. Because she was that kind of person, she was, indeed, more concerned about my welfare. That's why I loved her so much. I knew she missed Christopher, but I reassured her that everything would be fine.

The weeks past by and I had no contact from the Greek courts, nor any news of Christopher. I went back to work. I needed to do something to put Greece to the back of my mind for a while and wait for the decision. One afternoon, I received a phone call from my mother. Her voice was soft and gentle. "Ian, I'm sorry, but Christopher's not coming home. The Greek courts have decided he should stay in Greece with his mother."

I fell onto my chair and sobbed my heart out. The bombshell had devastated my world and for the next hour or so, I just stared through the windows of my office seeing nothing. My mind was totally blank and my head was somewhere beyond the horizon. I left the office and headed straight for the Balmoral pub in Bolton town centre. It was three o'clock in the afternoon and I stayed until last orders. I was very drunk, completely off my head. I drank myself into a state of oblivion to try to put Greece and all it stood for, out of my mind. I knew it would only be for a short while, but it still felt bloody good.

This drinking became a regular thing. I relied on the drink to get me through. I wasn't proud of what I was doing, but it was the only way I could get through the miserable days and the lonely nights. Most nights I was drunk and the weekends were the same. I tried to put Helen and Christopher and Greece behind me.

One weekend when I was out, I met Suzi. She was a lot younger than me - I was thirty-nine and Suzi was twenty-one. She was very pretty and slim with medium brown hair. I was attracted to her immediately and I liked her southern accent. She wasn't from Bolton originally. She came from Kent and had lived in Bolton for nearly three years. We started to see each other on a regular basis and I felt comfortable with her. In hindsight, I was probably on the rebound, but it was one way of getting over the pain of losing Helen and Christopher.

Suzi and I had of lot of fun together. She made me feel good and we were good together.

The local press latched onto the news of the abduction. They asked to meet me with a view to covering my story in the newspaper. I wasn't sure if I was ready to re-live it all again, but nevertheless I decided to meet with the editor of the Bolton Evening News. I discussed absolutely everything with him, how I met Helen, the beating I was given by Vangelis and his cronies, smuggling her out of Greece, the abduction and the ordeal in the Greek courts.

When he asked if I would like to go to Greece with a couple of reporters to cover her side of the story too, I wasn't sure. "You could see Christopher and we will pay for everything," he offered.

The thought of seeing Christopher again was like a carrot to a donkey. I considered the editor's offer and finally agreed to go to Greece. I would see Christopher and give him some Christmas presents. It was too good an opportunity to miss.

Chapter 17 – Taking BEN reporters to Greece.

I flew out to Greece in February 1999 with a reporter named Matthew Taylor and photographer, Nigel Taggart. The trip was arranged so that Matthew might get another angle on my story from Maria's point of view. That, in itself promised to be interesting. Matthew was a serious kind of guy, what I imagined an Oxford University graduate would be like - well mannered and academic. Nigel, on the other hand was bubbly and telling jokes all the time, but they were both good company and I was happy to travel with them.

When we landed in Athens, Matthew and Nigel were excited about their overseas project. It was their first trip abroad to cover a story for the Bolton Evening News. As for me, I didn't give a damn anymore about my trips to Greece. I felt battle weary and hardened by then. We stayed in an up-market hotel in Piraeus, all expenses paid as promised. Matthew and Nigel couldn't wait to get started. I knew what to expect after all my experiences in Greece, but I think they were oblivious to the whole situation. I did warn them about the dangers and what could happen to us all. My last trip in December 1998 after the last court case had not been a pleasant one, especially when I walked out on Helen. Refusing to drop the kidnapping charges had more than likely made the whole family deeply resentful.

We went to a local cafe I knew well and discussed our plan of action. I had to smile, not because I was happy with what we were about to do, more with an ironic acceptance that we might be facing more than they realised. Our trip to Greece was only for three days so Matthew and Nigel decided that the next day we would go to the house. The way they were talking, even after my warnings, they were totally unprepared for what might happen.

I sighed deeply. "Okay," I said shaking my head slowly. "Just be prepared for anything. These people don't react as we would. Expect the unexpected and you'll be all right."

For the rest of the day I showed them round Athens. I took them to historical Plaka and of course, I had to show them my favourite landmark, the Acropolis. They took pictures of me there and at various other places around Athens, photographs that would be published with the story in the newspaper. The publicity I was getting at home had intensified and the national press as well as television and radio stations wanted to interview me. Matthew and Nigel were enjoying the day and were more like tourists than reporters. In the evening we went for a meal in a restaurant on the harbour front in Piraeus. We ordered the best food and drink appreciating the generosity of the Bolton Evening News. We ate like kings and sampling a couple of bottles of the local wine simply added to a fantastic evening.

Back in the hotel, we further discussed the plan of action for the next day. "Be careful what you say," I warned them, "especially when you talk to Helen and Maria. If you bombard Helen with questions, she'll panic. Maria is the opposite. She'll find one little thing to turn around to make it look like you've been offensive to them and then you'll be in the lap of the gods."

"You are joking, aren't you?" they asked in unison.

"No, I'm not," I said firmly. "They'll be very nervous because they'll think we are there to snatch Christopher and take him back to England. They always thought I would try to do that before, so they'll think that's why we're here now, I'm sure. They are very wary of strangers so like I said before, expect the unexpected."

The following morning, Matthew and Nigel were obviously very excited about going to Helen's house. I repeated the instructions again. "Let me go to the house first and explain why you are here. I'll say you are friends of mine on your first trip to Athens. If you give them any clue that you are from the Press, Maria particularly won't like it. She will be absolutely terrified of bad publicity."

We caught a bus to Perama and got off at the bottom of the hill. I had thought I would never have to climb that hill again, but there I was and strangely, it wasn't an emotional journey for me. Nigel had his camera at the ready and Matthew had his notebook in his hand. When the house was in view, we stopped at my request and I pulled them to one side. "Don't forget," I reminded them earnestly. "You are friends of mine and you are taking pictures of me giving Christopher his Christmas presents. Let me speak to Helen and Maria first before you take any pictures, or ask any questions." I repeated to them they must not say they were reporters. I told them again, "I'll tell Helen you are taking the photographs for me to keep. I want them to make an album of Christopher while he's here in Greece."

I hoped Matthew and Nigel would do as I asked. "How will I get the information I need for the piece in the paper?" Matthew asked. "That's the whole point of being here."

I thought for a minute. "If I ask the questions, she'll think it's just me asking again why she lied in court. I'll let her think I'm still hurting from the bad things she said." That wasn't a million miles from the truth, because I still felt sad when I thought about it.

Just before I went to up to the house, Granada Television news rang me. They wanted me to do a telephone interview which would be broadcast on the news that went out on the evening show. They were asking me about the abduction and about my visit to Greece. I answered as clearly as I was able under the circumstances. In truth, it wasn't a good time, but I coped.

As we approached the house, Maria was on the balcony and she saw us as we climbed up the stairs. Both Maria and

Helen opened the door. "Who are these men?" Helen asked warily.

"They are friends of mine who I met in Bolton. This is their first time in Greece so I'm showing them around," I reassured her.

"Why has he got a camera?" Maria asked pointing at Nigel.

"All tourists have cameras, Maria," I said sarcastically. "I want him to take my photograph when I give Christopher his Christmas presents. I am going to make an album so I can look at Christopher's photos when I miss him."

Maria looked perturbed. "I know why you're here and if you think you can snatch Christopher and take him away, think again," she said with bravado.

"I'm only here for a few days and I want to give Christopher his presents," I said again.

"Only you are coming in," she stated harshly. "I don't know those two and I don't trust them." She glared at Matthew and Nigel.

I was just about to step through the doorway when Nigel pulled his camera out and started to take pictures of the angry Maria. That was red rag to a bull and she slammed the door in my face. "I'm calling the police," she shouted.

Quickly, I turned to the guys and told them to leave. "Get out of here!" I instructed urgently. "The police don't hang about and they'll be here in a minute." Just then I saw Christopher on the balcony. When I caught his eye, I called up to him. "I love you, Chris. I love you very much."

Nigel carried on taking the pictures as newspaper photographers do. I could see the police car racing up the hill. "Hurry up, you two," I called out, trying to make them accept the urgency of the situation. "Give me the films."

They quickly took the films out of the camera and threw them to me. "Take them back to the hotel and don't let anybody see them. We need to get the photographs in the paper."

I scarpered quickly like a bat out of hell and made my way back to the hotel. I went straight in to my room and hid the films in my socks. Within a few minutes, the phone rang. It was the Editor of the Bolton Evening News. "Have you got the films?" he asked.

"I have," I answered. "How did you know I had them?"

"Thanks, Ian. You've done well. Keep them safe, but I have received a call from Matthew," he told me. "He and Nigel have been arrested and put in the cells. Apparently, your mother-in-law wants them charged under the Privacy Act."

"Oh my God!" I said. "I'll have to find out what's happening."

I went immediately to the police station in Perama, the same one where I broke down crying when Christopher was abducted. To my surprise, Remanos, the police sergeant and my old friend was at the desk. He shook my hand and hugged me which made me feel more at ease. "Are Matthew and Nigel in the cells," I asked him tentatively.

Remanos smiled and said they were, but first he would explain to me the implications of the Privacy Act. "Listen carefully, Ian," he said seriously. "The Privacy Act is a law in Greece where you are not allowed to take pictures or videos without the person's permission. If you do, it might end in a prosecution. You could face three months in prison and then get deported."

My heart was beating fast in my chest and I was shit-scared again. I hadn't felt like that since the Yugoslavian police had slowly checked our passports at the border when I was helping Helen escape from Greece, but this information might have worse consequences for me. "What can I do, Remanos?" I asked, not hiding the panic I was feeling. "I can't get deported. I have to get back into Greece to see Christopher. Bloody hell!" I was very nervous and apprehensive as I didn't know what was facing me.

"Maria has complained to the police that you tried to force your way into her house uninvited and you were taking pictures without their permission,' he told me, "and you were also being abusive towards her and Helen."

I told Remanos they were lying as usual and were deliberately trying to get me into trouble.

"Sit down, Ian," he said quietly. "You must sign these papers."

It was a charge sheet. We were all being charged under the Privacy Act, but Remanos didn't appear to be unduly concerned. "Don't worry," he reassured me. "I'll help you as much as I can." He smiled warmly. "Wait here. I won't be a moment." He put on the television so that I could watch a video while he was away. What appeared on the screen was very unexpected. I was watching a pornographic movie. I couldn't believe it! Matthew and Nigel were locked up in a cell and here was I, watching a porno.

Remanos returned carrying a tray with four glasses of beer on it. We grinned at other and we had a couple of drinks and a laugh. Poor Matthew and Nigel were still locked up and I didn't intend telling them I was having a good time while they were locked up in police cells for hours. That would really rub salt in the wound.

Little did I know at the time that our escapade had made the news back home. They reported that all three of us were locked up in the police cells and were facing a prison sentence and deportation. I understood why they had said that. At nine o'clock that evening, Nigel and Matthew were let out of the cells. Remanos had received a phone call from an embassy official and we were told we were free to leave, but had to return at a later date to face the Greek court. Matthew and Nigel looked worse for wear. I winked at Remanos and said goodbye. The booze and the porno would remain our secret, but mean though it might appear, I couldn't help chuckling to myself.

We left Greece the following day and reports of the events were put to press. I appeared with my mother on Granada television the same night. When I was interviewed on live television, they mentioned the fact we were all arrested, implying to the viewers on that it was an ordeal for us. I tried my best not to smile.

I saw Matthew and Nigel many times over the years as my story was frequently in the press. They both said they would never go to Greece again. I just smiled. I didn't dare tell them the real truth. Much to the relief of us all, none of us were charged and the case was dropped. For me, every journey to Greece was full of twist and turns. I never knew what was in store for me and nothing surprised me anymore.

Chapter 18 – Diane fighting my corner.

The date for our appeal was in June 1999. My sister, Diane was accompanying me this time. Mum and Jack felt it best because Diane was young and confident with a strong personality. She would certainly cope with anything Maria and Co would throw at her. Diane and I stayed at my mum and Jack's the night before we were flying out to Greece. We went out for a family meal in Farnworth. We tucked into good, wholesome Lancashire food – just what we needed before we left to continue the fight to bring Christopher home.

We spoke about our experiences on our last visit to Greece. We all agreed that the highlight was seeing Christopher and what happened in the court room didn't warrant much of our time discussing it. We had to laugh at Jack going on about KFC and how he loved it.

Jack's conversation nearly always included food and how he had loved the Kentucky fried chicken in Omonia Square in Athens. It was a pleasant evening and we had a good laugh and a good night out.

Diane is a very intelligent woman and as tough as they come. With her around, I wasn't worried about facing Maria or Vangelis as I knew Diane would put them in their place if needs be. We flew out to Greece with a Daily Express reporter named Melvyn Jones. We hoped it would be a successful trip and we set out full of hope and expectation. Melvyn was a very serious guy and very well-educated. He was also very experienced reporter who had covered stories all over Europe. It had only been a few months since my last trip to Greece, with the two reporters from the Bolton Evening News. Getting arrested and charged under the privacy laws after a confrontation with Helen's family, had not been on our agenda. With that in mind, I had a good idea that this trip might be a difficult one.

Melvyn stayed in Athens, but Diane and I stayed in a place called Agia Marina on a Greek Island called Aegina. It was a beautiful island with sandy beaches, plenty of bars and cafés and a place steeped in history.

For the first couple of days, Diane and I chilled out and relaxed in the bars near the beach. We kept in touch with Melvyn, but we didn't plan to meet up with him till the morning of the appeal in Piraeus. We needed to relax and forget about the up-coming court appearance which we both knew would be difficult and challenging. Diane was struggling with the heat and she was getting bitten by mosquitoes on a daily basis. I remember that one night, she was cocooned in her bed sheet with only her nose sticking out so she wouldn't get bitten. She looked so comical and I couldn't stop laughing especially in the morning when she woke up. Her face and arms were still covered in bites so her plan of action obviously hadn't worked. I tried my best not to laugh out loud, but it was very difficult. Diane wasn't amused at all.

Diane and I were very close and we were very protective of each other. She was only small, but she was a pit-bull terrier if anybody upset her. Maybe it's true what they say about red hair and fiery tempers. That would describe Diane to a tee, but she was very loving and caring and I always looked up to her as she was a few years older than me.

After we had had our fun, the time came for us to be serious and it was the morning of the appeal. We met up with Melvyn who took notes about all that had happened previously. It wasn't long before my lawyer arrived – my very pretty, but completely inefficient lawyer who had badly let down my mother and me in the previous courts cases. I wasn't allowed to have my own British lawyer, because the rules were that I must use the Greek justice lawyer even though I considered she wasn't up to the job.

Helen was represented by a top lawyer that cost thousands of drachmas; so in my opinion it was no contest. I felt defeated before I began. A top lawyer against my inexperienced and inefficient young lawyer didn't give me much of a chance. I hated being negative, but that's how I felt.

We waited for Helen and her lawyer to turn up, but surprise, surprise! They didn't arrive.

I was so angry. It was becoming a total farce. Melvyn had all ready seen all our evidence which proved everything Helen and Vangelis had said at the last hearing were lies. I had documented evidence to prove that. I could see Melvyn was getting annoyed especially when my Greek so-called lawyer said the appeal court would look at my wife's evidence then look at mine and make a decision in five months time. Helen's lawyer had already handed her evidence in to the judge and mine was sent to The Lord Chancellor's office six weeks before They had sent it to the Greek Chancellor's office and all my documents had to be translated which cost me a bloody fortune. I also had copies of all my documents and evidence translated into Greek as I was very suspicious of the Greek legal system.

Diane was livid with my lawyer. She yelled at her at the top of her voice. "What about the court case?"

"There will be no court case as Helen and her lawyer haven't turned up so they cannot proceed," my lawyer replied. "The appeal judges will look at both sides of the evidence behind closed doors and you we will be notified about the decision in four to five months."

She then walked off.

Melvyn was disgusted. "This is a set up and sounds like the system is corrupt," he said not hiding his annoyance. Later, he and I went for a drink in a local bar in Piraeus. It was a small family bar which wasn't usually packed out, so we were able to discuss the day's events in peace and without being interrupted.

"This is just typical of Helen," I told him. "She will be hoping that by not turning up I will run out of money and give up the fight for Christopher. It will also prolong Christopher's stay in Greece knowing full well he is getting used to the Greek culture and way of life."

Melvyn shook his head in disbelief and said, "Under international law, the child must be returned to the country of residence and the courts in that country will decide what is best for him. He told me he would write a piece in his newspaper about the diabolical way we were being treated and how Greece was not following international law. I could see in his eyes that he felt sorry for me and he advised me to see my local Member of Parliament to take my case to European Court of Human Rights. "Good luck," he said before he left. "Be strong and carry on the fight forced upon you by a blatant miscarriage of justice." That was the last we saw, or heard of Melvyn, but he did send me copies of the newspaper that carried the story about our time Greece.

Diane decided we should go to Helen's house. "We have come all this way," she said firmly, "and we should go and see them." I didn't argue with her even though there would definitely be a confrontation with Helen's mother after the fiasco last time. However, I did feel safe with Diane as she is the kind of person who takes no prisoners and was more than a match for Maria.

We caught the green bus to Perama. The journey was second nature to me. We got off at the bus top at the bottom of the hill and I felt it best to warn her about the long, steep hill to Helen's house. It took us a while, not because we were feeling the strain of the climb, but because Diane was fascinated by the houses we passed. She was curious to know how the Greeks lived.

"I have a lot of memories of this hill, good and bad," I told her. "I call it the hill of tears."

Diane smiled. "Forget the past now and just think of seeing Christopher.

I smiled at her and I said, "You know, Diane, you are my pride and joy. I couldn't ask for a better sister."

"I should think not!" she quipped.

We arrived at the house and I saw Helen and Maria on the balcony. We climbed up the steps and I whispered to Diane, "This is where Maria threw my suitcase down the stairs and told me my marriage was over and I wouldn't see Helen and Christopher again."

Diane replied. "Don't you worry about Maria; I'll put her in her place. Just watch me." She was the fearless avenger, determined and strong, but I have to admit even though I was battle-hardened, my legs were like jelly and Diane took the lead.

Maria opened the door and Diane said, "Hello," as she pushed straight passed her without an invitation to go in. I followed her without looking at sour-faced Maria. We just sat down and I watched Diane in admiration. She was straight-faced and she was giving out the orders to bring Christopher to us while she sat there with her arms folded. There she was in the lion's den and she was telling Helen and Maria what to do in no uncertain terms. I looked at Maria and she was very nervous. She shouted to Helen to go and get Christopher and like a little lamb, she obeyed.

Christopher was quite shy at first. He was nervous and I knew he would be afraid of showing his love and affection towards us and towards me in particular. The poor child had obviously suffered emotionally. I could sense it and I felt sure he would have been brain-washed by his mother and Vangelis all these months. Diane settled him down quickly by talking to him and playing with him. Soon he responded and hugged Diane. I went and sat down next to him. I told him I would never leave him and I would always love him. With that, he went into his bed room and came back with a candle and a CD with some games on, so I could play on his play station.

I could see Maria getting upset, because Christopher was showing me love and affection.

He told me he loved me and missed me. Maria went into the kitchen and came out with a cup of whipped egg yolk and tried to feed Christopher. That riled Diane. She took the bowl from Maria and said bluntly, "He's eight years old, not a baby. Go in the kitchen and make him some proper food."

I don't know how I kept myself from laughing out loud, but I couldn't hide the broad grin on my face. I looked at Maria and she was as white as a sheet. I looked at Helen and she said nothing. I was so proud of Diane. She took no crap from anybody and I was glad she was on my side. Diane knew of all the heartbreak Helen and her family had caused my mum and me and now it was pay-back big time.

Christopher came out with a ball and by accident he knocked a vase over and smashed it. I knew Maria would blow her top and she did just that. I knew from past experience she was so house-cleaning crazy. She was always cleaning and if we ever dropped a crumb, she would clean it up straight away. She would even get the creases out of the couch when we stood up and the same with the bed sheets when we got out of bed. Most bizarre of all, she would iron Vangelis' underwear! She was crazy! Anyway, back to the broken vase. Maria got hold of Christopher and started to shout at him. I was just going to say something when Diane jumped up and shouted at Maria, "If you ever shout at Christopher like that again, I'll break more than a vase! Leave the child alone."

Maria went red in the face and to my surprise, she let go of Christopher and walked away into the bedroom. I was revelling in it and I thought to myself, *any small victory is a bonus.*

Maria surely has met her match.

At that point, Helen started to open up and began chatting to both Diane and me. Out of the blue and very unexpectedly, Diane said, "Why did you do it? How can you live here like this with that crazy mother of yours?"

Helen just shrugged her shoulders. I knew she was influenced by her family. I could see the sadness in her eyes, but I was determined not to show any feelings or emotions to her.

We stayed for about an hour and the time I spent with Christopher was very precious. I kissed him goodbye and asked Helen if we could visit again the next day. She agreed and we saw Christopher and Helen a few times before we went home. Every time we were there, Maria sensibly kept out of our way.

We said our goodbyes to Christopher. I was sad to leave him again, but I promised myself I would never give up my fight for my son. We left the house and I hugged Diane. "I am so proud of you," I told her.

"I have dealt with worse things in my life." She replied with a smile. "Maria doesn't scare me." This brought a big smile to my face. I felt very safe with Diane. "Now it's time to sort out another problem," she said and she winked. "Let's get to that lawyer's office."

The lawyer's office was in Piraeus. When we arrived, Diane stormed up the stairs and straight into the office with me tagging along behind. My lawyer could not have anticipated facing Diane's wrath. "Don't look so surprised," Diane hissed like a venomous snake. "My brother needed your expertise and what did you give him?" The young lawyer just stood there wide-eyed and visibly shaken. Before she could respond to the onslaught, Diane continued. "Call yourself a lawyer?" She asked, not waiting for an answer. "You are as corrupt as the mafia and a waste of time. In short, you are a useless bitch with no brains. In my opinion, you would be more suited to working in a supermarket." Enough said. We walked out of her office in military fashion and headed to the nearest bar.

I could hardly believe Diane had sorted out Maria and my lawyer in a matter of hours, something I hadn't been able to do in all my visits to Greece.

We returned to the Aegina and we spent the last few days having a laugh and a good time.

During the day we spent time on the beach just relaxing and going for a swim. It was the last time Diane ever visited Greece. I thought that was a pity, because she was game for anything and fun to be with. When we flew back to England, we laughed all the way home. My big sister had sorted out Maria and I intended to celebrate her victory in the Bolton bars over the following days.

After that eventful visit to Greece, I carried on with my life for a few months seeing Suzi. She and I grew very close and she was a great comfort to me. I went back to work with a smile on my face. As for Diane, we regularly keep in touch and we still laugh about the way she put Maria in her place.

A few weeks later, I received a letter from the Lord Chancellor's Office which stated that my sister, Diane had to apologise in writing to my lawyer or they wouldn't continue with my case in Greece. Diane wrote a letter saying she was sorry, but only because it may affect any court cases in the future. Diane was still stubborn till the very end. I enjoyed my journey to Greece with her and I knew she was only protecting me against what we both considered the inefficiencies of the Greek legal system. She was a fighter and caring at the same time and she went to Greece to be by my side, something for which I shall always be truly grateful.

Chapter 19 – Support from everybody.

After I returned to England, I settled into normality, or whatever passed for normality and I tried to forget all the heartbreak of the recent events in Greece. I carried on seeing Suzi as we grow very close over the last few months. She was very understanding and caring and helped me overcome the pain of losing Helen and Christopher. She knew everything about Christopher and Helen, not just from the press and television, but also from me as I was very honest with her from the start.

Suzi and I went out together regularly and we also went for a week's holiday in The Algarve. We loved Portugal and stayed in Praia da Rocha, a busy resort which attracts families, groups and couples due to its good selection of attractions and amenities. There were plenty of bars, restaurants, nightclubs and not forgetting the famous beachfront casino. As well as the great beaches, there was plenty to do in the area such as water parks, water sports. It suited us perfectly and we had a fantastic time during which we grew very close. Greece was put on the back burner for a while. We knew we needed a week without thinking about it.

On our return to England, I received a letter from the Lord Chancellor's Office in London stating that the decision could not be overturned. I wasn't shocked at all as I had already realised that the system in Greece at that time was corrupt. At home, I was recognised all the time, no matter where I went and offers to appear on television and the radio were coming almost every day. I sat down with my mum and Jack and asked what they thought I should do with my life after all the upheaval. "Do you think I will be able to carry on with the fight? It seems to me I'm fighting a losing battle."

They lifted my spirits and telling me, "You must carry on with your fight for yourself, for your family and especially for Christopher."

I looked at my mum with glazed eyes. I was tired of all the fighting with Helen's family. It seemed to have lasted a lifetime, but knowing I had the support of my family, I was persuaded to carry on. In a strange kind of way, I felt I could deal with anything they threw at me and was ready for the battles to commence again, especially with the blessing of my mum and Jack.

I made an appointment to see my local European MP Gary Titley and explained about the problems with the Greek courts and the way I was treated. I was surprised to find out that he had already been following my story and he took my case to the European Court of Human Rights.

In the meantime, I was receiving letters of support from all over the country. Dorothy Martland helped me to set up a Christopher Lomax Appeal Fund to help me fund my trips to Greece. Dorothy was Helen's friend, but she was also mine. She was a lovely, kind-hearted person and so was her husband, Alan. They ran the local Market Radio station in Bolton where Helen worked for a while. We printed leaflets and when we asked for them to be displayed, the local shops and my local bank were very understanding. They willingly put the leaflets in their windows and even had collection boxes to help me raise some money for the appeal. The Daily Express and the Bolton Evening News as well as the television programme, Granada Reports, all helped me.

The people of Bolton were fantastic. They helped me through the difficult times I was going through. A group of pensioners in an old people's home had a jumble sale and the money they made went to the appeal fund. Things like that really touched my heart. A local club owner had a charity evening in his night club and I appreciated that very much.

The club in question was Club Mondo in Bolton. Dorothy, my sister Pat and I attended the charity night. People, male and female, as young as eighteen contributed. One person gave me a framed Bolton Wanderers shirt which had been signed by all the players. It was sold in an auction for nearly two hundred pounds. The charity night raised over five hundred pounds for which I was very grateful. The generosity and kindness of the people of Bolton was more than I could have ever expected and the support they gave me will always be a very special memory for me.

The phone calls to Christopher continued. I taped some of them, because I sensed his family was next to him, telling him what to say to. Some of the things he said were very hurtful, but I ignored them as I knew it wasn't Christopher's fault. He was saying things like, "English people are evil and the country is cold. You have thrown all my toys away..." I felt Maria was behind all this and I hated her with a passion. Christopher was being brain-washed and I felt so sorry for him. It was so cruel and typical of Maria to use him just to get back at me.

I was more determined than ever to wipe that smile off her face just like Diane had done. I started my fight back by launching a petition in Bolton. I had a stall in the middle of Bolton town centre with a board displaying all the press cuttings about my case. I had three books where anybody could sign their names in support of my fight. I received more than five thousand signatures. I had all kinds of people signing from young children to the aged and from all different nationalities. It was a very successful day and it warmed my heart to see all the support I was getting from all kinds of backgrounds. It was the support I received from the people of Bolton and my family and friends which helped me to get through the nightmare and helped me to gain the strength to carry on the fight, not just against Helen and her family, but also against the miscarriage of justice I believed I had received in the Greek courts.

One morning I heard a letter drop through my letter box. When I opened it, I clearly saw in black and white, a hearing to fight for access was set for May 2000. It had been a whole year since I had last seen Christopher so I was looking forward to going to Greece to fight once again for justice. They had to allow me to see my son.

Chapter 20 – The appeal.

In April 2000, my new partner, Suzi and I prepared to fly out to Greece again for the access appeal. We stayed in, the night before the morning flight to Athens. Previously, I had made a point of going out the night before we left, but this time I wanted to talk to Suzi and make sure she was comfortable with the situation. She already knew what had been happening as I had been honest with her from the start of our relationship. She wanted to go to Greece and give me support.

I had told Suzi everything about the courts and the way my mother and I were treated so she would know what to expect from Helen if they ever met up. "Don't worry about me, Ian," she said gently. "I'll be with you all the way, the ups and downs, through thick and thin and I'll do whatever I can to help you win your appeal."

The appeal would be the best chance for me to gain access to see Christopher as there had been a lot of interest in the case, especially because my European MP, Gary Titley, had brought it to the attention of the European Parliament in

Brussels as well as the publicity I had received in England. The European Court of Human Rights had taken an interest in my case.

I made sure I had all my evidence in case it had gone missing in the Greek system. I still didn't trust them and I had to be prepared for anything. I was ready for the fight of my life. I was stronger now and more determined than ever to see my son who I had fought for, for so long.

I had lost all my other court cases and I was not going to lose this one. Helen and especially Maria and Vangelis will see a big difference in me. They would never again see a broken man in court who allowed himself to shed the tears of depression and fear of losing his son. They would never again see a man who was weak because of the love he had for Helen; the man who was afraid of losing her. I will never forgive them for the hurt and pain they had inflicted on me. I loved Christopher and I would fight like never before to get justice to see my son. I wanted to get the ultimate revenge against Helen, her mother and Vangelis which I had craved for so long.

Suzi and I stayed on the Greek Island of Aegina in the same place my sister and I had stayed the year before. I had made a few friends there especially Mike, whose dad owned a bar. My Bolton Wanderers top took pride of place among all the other football tops which adorned the walls of Mike's bar. We spent several nights there drinking into the early hours with Mike and his family.

It was Suzi's first of many trips to Greece and a trip she wouldn't forget in a hurry. We stayed in a hotel called The Oasis. It was a very old hotel, but very quaint and traditional which was typical of most of the hotels on the island. We arrived there in the late afternoon and it was still very hot which was to my liking. Aegina is a small, beautiful island which has easy access from Piraeus on the mainland. The trip by boat usually took about an hour. The island had many bars and plenty of restaurants serving traditional food. In summer, it was usually visited by mainly Greeks for weekend visits to get away from the hustle and bustle of Athens. I loved it and I knew Suzi would love it too.

For the first couple of days we just relaxed and I showed Suzi around the island. In the evenings, we drank the night away in Mike's bar till the early hours. Mike kept giving us shots and homemade cocktails and to this day I don't know what Mike put in them. I got so drunk one night, I fell over, smashed a table and cut my head open. I vowed I would never again drink Mike's homemade cocktails. I stuck to the local beer after that. I needed to remember my reason for being there and keep a clear head.

The first visit we had to make was to the International Social Services in Athens. There we met a social worker who was to act as mediator between Helen and me to try to reach some middle ground in Christopher's best interest. The social worker was concerned about what psychological damage it might do to Christopher after all the court battles and infighting between both parents. It couldn't have been good for him. On our second visit to Social Services, Helen was there. The social worker made clear to her the importance that a child needed both parents. Helen was told she must try to get used to the idea as the judge may well give access visits to me. "Ian's role is vital in the upbringing of Christopher," she said. "You have to accept that."

Helen wasn't at all happy with the idea of me having any kind of access visits and she made that pretty clear to the social worker. True to form, Helen caused an almighty fuss and the social worker ended the meeting. I didn't go to International Social Services again. I realised that Helen intended to fight tooth and nail in the court to stop me gaining access to my son. It gave me a clear warning that I was going to have a fight on my hands, yet again.

Suzi and I arrived at the court early and we met up with my lawyer soon afterwards. I was nervous when meeting her again as I didn't know what kind of reception I would get after the tongue-lashing she had received from my sister, Diane. It was embarrassing to think of it, but my lawyer seemed determined and surprisingly, her manner was very friendly and warm towards me. I couldn't help but think that Diane had done me a favour and my lawyer had realised she hadn't really fought for me previously. I will never know the truth about that, but I was happy with her so far.

My lawyer took Suzi and me into a small room and told us that we would have a good chance of getting access, but only in Greece at the moment. All my evidence had been assessed by the judge and she said, "I'm pretty sure you will get some kind of access visits."

For the first time I felt confident with my lawyer who I had previously thought was out of her depth. She had given me hope. As we left the room, I saw Helen with Vangelis and her lawyer. We were advised by my lawyer to ignore them.

Suzi couldn't resist getting one over on Helen and she calmly handed her an envelope containing the divorce papers. Helen glared as she opened the envelope. "I'm not signing these," she said bitterly, but Suzi only had to serve the papers to Helen. As long as she had received them, the divorce would go through.

Helen was furious and threw the papers back at Suzi who carried on walking with a huge smile on her face. Round one to me, I thought with a smile.

We went into court and sat down. My lawyer introduced us to our translator who was called Demetrius. The court room was empty, not like the last time when it had been like a cattle market. It seemed like I was dreaming. Everything was completely different. I had a lawyer who was completely transformed and we had an interpreter who spoke fluent English. The judge arrived in court and the hearing was about to begin.

It was a different judge from the last time and I could see him looking at Suzi and me, then at Helen and Vangelis. Both lawyers approached the judge and gave both sets of papers to him. My lawyer smiled and sat in front of me. The battle was about to commence and the judge asked for Vangelis to step up to the bench.

"What kind of relationship do you have with the boy, Christopher?" he asked.

"A good one," Vangelis answered. "I treat him like my own son."

I couldn't argue with that. I knew Vangelis treated Christopher well.

"Have you ever visited England?" the judge asked.

I waited for Vangelis answer.

"Yes," Vangelis lied.

"You have stated here that Christopher's father is a criminal with a drink problem and he abused his wife and child," the judge stated as he read the documents in front of him.

"Yes, it's true," Vangelis lied again. "He was unemployed in England and he stole a car."

I was astounded by what he was saying and I wanted to stand up and shout – Liar! You dirty rotten liar! – But I restrained myself. I would get my turn later.

Finally, the judge asked Vangelis, "Did you support Ian Lomax, his wife and his son when they were in England?"

"Yes, I did," Vangelis lied yet again. The evil bastard turned round to me and smiled shamelessly.

His despicable actions weren't missed by the judge who demanded, "Sit down."

Vangelis was angry. "Sit down?" he shouted at the judge. "I have questions and I need answers. I'm not sitting down until I say my piece."

The judge was having none of it and politely, yet forcefully he demanded again, "Sit down, please."

I could see Vangelis was becoming flustered and so was his lawyer. Vangelis had just been stopped from making us listen to his lies and he was livid. When he sat down, I winked at him and smiled. I nodded slowly in his direction. It was pay-back time.

Next up was Helen. She was dressed like she was for the second court case, scruffy and with no make-up. It was so obvious she was trying to give the impression she was ill with worrying about losing Christopher. I could read her like a book.

The judge didn't mess about and he asked her, "Do you object to Christopher's father having access?"

"Yes, I do," Helen replied. "If he is given access it must be supervised. I would allow him only half an hour and I must be there all the time."

Surprisingly, the judge cut her short. "Sit down." Her lawyer was disgusted and it showed in the way he was glaring at everybody. As for me, I considered the judge had read our documents thoroughly and it was looking good.

Suzi was the next to be called and I could see complete shock on Helens face. She had no idea what was going on, but I knew that Suzi was going to be my star witness. We had decided to fight fire with fire and Helen and Vangelis would get a taste of their own medicine.

The judge was very polite with Suzi. "Can you tell the court what your life was like in England when Helen and Christopher were living there?" he asked.

Suzi smiled and nodded. "I used to be their babysitter. Helen was a good mother and Ian was a good father," she explained. "They had a lovely house and they used to go on holidays regularly."

"Were you there when Vangelis visited them?" the judged asked.

"Vangelis was never there," Suzi told him. "Only Maria visited England when Ian and Helen went to Paris. She looked after Christopher while they were away."

I turned round to look at Helen and Vangelis. Helen was furious and shouted, "She is lying. I don't know her. She has never been our babysitter."

The judge raised his eyebrows and looked at Helen. "Be quiet or leave the court," he instructed and Helen glared at me as she sat down. I was full of confidence by then as everything seemed to be going our way.

"I'm sorry about the interruption," the judge apologised to Suzi. "You may sit down now and thank you."

When it was my turn to face, I felt full of confidence. The judge smiled as he asked, "Mr Lomax, do you love Christopher?"

"Very much," I replied.

"It is very clear that you love him and that is why you are here to gain access to see him. Am I right in saying this?" the judge continued.

"Yes and I want to be able to see him as often as possible," I told him.

"Would you be happy to visit Christopher in Greece?" he asked gently.

"I want to spend some time with my son no matter where or how little time as long as I can see him, because I love and miss him very much," I said. I knew I was pleading, but I needed to make sure the judge knew how genuine I was in my appeal for access.

"Do you keep in contact with your son by letter or telephone?" he asked.

"Yes, every week without fail," I told him.

"Thank you. You may now sit down," he said and smiled at me.

Both lawyers had to approach the bench. I couldn't hear what was going on, but my interpreter told me that the judge had given me some unsupervised access in Greece for the present, but he didn't know how much. My lawyer returned and sat next to me. "Congratulations," she said. "You have won some unsupervised access in Greece for now, but the judge has to decide how much you will get."

Suddenly all my emotions just came out and I began to cry. I hugged Suzi. My feelings were indescribable. I just couldn't believe I finally won. I had finally got my revenge. I hugged my lawyer and thanked her in full view of the judge. I glanced at him and I detected the hint of a smile on his face as if to say well done. Helen and Vangelis stormed out of the court room.

My lawyer told me her office would get in touch with the Lord Chancellor's Office with the decision about my access rights within six weeks. "If you would like to know before then, you could travel to the Greek court in three weeks time and the information will be available." She gave me a translation of part of the judgement given to her by the judge and pointed out to me a reference number at the top of the page. "You will have to show this to the office in the court building."

I shook hands with my lawyer and she wished me good luck. "Goodbye," she said. "I hope all goes well for you and Christopher." I watched her leave the building and wondered why she hadn't fought like that in the earlier court cases, but all that didn't matter anymore.

When Suzi and I left the court building, Helen was waiting for us on her own. Vangelis had disappeared. She came over to me and asked, "Why did Suzi lie in court?"

I stared at her wide-eyed. "Do you mean to say you don't know?" I asked her pointedly. "We only did the same as you and Vangelis did. You said I was a thief and that I abused you and Christopher. I never stole car. How stupid can you get? I couldn't even drive and Vangelis has never been to England or supported us. And you dare to question why Suzi said she was our babysitter! Now, get lost. We are going to celebrate our victory."

Suzi and I headed for the nearest bar to celebrate. On the way there, I shouted at the top of my voice and punched the air. "Yeeeeeees!" I jumped up in the air and shouted, "Whoopee! Whoopee!" I was so very, very happy. Suzi was laughing her socks off and most of the passing Greeks just looked at me in puzzlement. I didn't care. I was enjoying my victory and why not? I had suffered for far too long at the hands of Helen's family. I didn't care how Helen and Vangelis were feeling. I would never forgive them for the hurt and pain they had caused, but I loved Christopher and I would fight all over again in order to be allowed to see my son.

We arrived back on Aegina still wallowing in our victory. The rest of the trip would be spent celebrating. We went straight to Mike's bar and showed him the translation. When he read it, he was surprised that I had only got access in

Greece, but I didn't care. I was glad I could be a father to him again.

The last few days on Aegina saw me a changed man. I was happy and all the hurt had disappeared. I decided it was all right for me to get drunk. I wanted enjoy my happiness for the first time since Christopher was stolen from my life. I called my mum to tell her the good news. She burst into tears and I knew what it meant to her. I also called the Bolton Evening News and told them of my victory. It was hot off the press the following night and I'm felt sure the people of Bolton were happy for me.

Suzi and I had to return home, but three weeks later we returned to Greece to obtain the directives from the court in Athens. We needed to get them translated into English in order to know what they contained. We studied it afterwards and found out that the judge had awarded me unsupervised access for weekends; every second Wednesday, Easter, Christmas and four weeks during the summer. I had as much contact as I wanted by letter or by telephone. Reading the small print, I discovered I didn't need to hand in my passport at the police station in Perama. If Helen didn't hand over Christopher at the British Embassy at the required time, she might be arrested and taken back to court.

It s seemed to me that after all the bad publicity about Greece, the miscarriage of justice and Gary Titley taking my case to the European Court of Human Rights, my last court case was just a formality. My lawyer had proved her worth and I had what I wanted - my son back in my life.

Before I left, I met Helen with Christopher on the park in Perama where I used to take Christopher to play. I showed her the papers and she started to cry. For a split second, I felt sorry for her, but that's all it was, a split second. I had suffered at the hands of her and her family and it was time for me now to enjoy my victory. It had been a long time coming.

"You and Vangelis destroyed my mother in court with your vicious lies and now you must suffer yourselves from the web of lies and deceit you have concocted all along." I was determined to tell her what she needed to know. "Don't think I didn't know what you were up to with the abduction and everything. I just didn't know how to deal with it at the time, because I truly loved you. In return for my love, you filled my life with pain. You were aided and abetted by your mother who threw me out of the house and told me I would never see you or Christopher again." I paused and looked her squarely in the eye. "You can thank Maria for giving me the strength to fight my cause. There was no way I was going to allow you, her or Vangelis to stop me from seeing my son. I sincerely hope that one day she will get her come-uppance for the sins she has committed, if not in this life, then in the next." They were harsh words, but well deserved and well meant.

All this time, Suzi sat quietly near to us, but Helen didn't look at her once. I continued to speak plainly to Helen. "I loved you dearly, but you have lost all the love I had for you. All the beautiful memories we shared have been destroyed by your deceit and lies. I don't think I shall ever forget all the pain and suffering you put me through, but I intend to have a good life without you."

I walked away from Helen and went to hug Christopher. "I love you so much, Chris. Don't let anybody tell you otherwise. Now I can be your father properly. I can hold you and kiss you and say I love without any outside interference." I kissed him and said good bye. "I'll see you soon," and I smiled at him.

Christopher smiled back. "See yer, Dad."

I walked away with Suzi down the hill of tears where all the memories, good and bad, would now become a distant memory. I flew back to England this time, not as broken man next to two empty seats, but with a new partner and a new future. I was beginning a new chapter in my life, all coming about because of my love for Christopher.

Chapter 21 – Being a father again

I was counting the days for my first access visit to see Christopher in Greece. I was so happy and excited. I just couldn't wait to hold him in my arms again. It had been a long and painful journey. The fighting in the Greek courts had left me totally drained emotionally. I would never deny that I loved Helen. She is the mother of my son. That part of my life will always be special to me. I fell in love and it's not a crime. I often wonder why it all turned sour, I have started a new chapter in my life and I have a new partner in Suzi. I finally divorced Helen and it was time to move on. Suzi and I cemented our relationship in October 2000. Suzi had been my shoulder to cry on and had comforted me through the difficult times. Now she was my wife and I loved her very much.

The night before we were flying out to see Christopher, Suzi and I went to visit my mother and Jack. My mother wanted to give me a letter for Christopher so she could tell him how much he was loved and missed. She also gave me a couple of little presents for him. "I don't want him to forget us," she said.

I couldn't sleep that night. I was like a child on Christmas Eve too excited to sleep. I lost count of the cups of coffee I drank and in the early hours of the morning, I went for a walk to calm my nerves. The suitcases were packed and an extra suitcase was taken full of presents and photos of me and my family; some of me and Christopher too. He would enjoy looking at them and seeing his relations in England.

We arrived at Manchester airport nice and early. The flight to Greece was a happy one for a change. We were both totally relaxed and I frequently checked my watch as I couldn't wait to land. We had arranged for Helen to drop Christopher off outside the British Embassy in Athens. It was used as a neutral area and stated as a requirement in the access order. It had been stipulated by the Greek authorities for our protection. We arranged to meet at one o'clock, but we arrived early so we could watch as Christopher saw us and cherish the moment. I recalled that I had broken down and cried at the British Embassy after Christopher's abduction in August 1998. This time I knew I would be crying for completely different reasons.

By two o'clock, they hadn't arrived. I was becoming very worried at the thought of Helen not turning up at all. Suzi reassured me and said we could go to the police station with our access order if she didn't arrive soon. Helen might very well be arrested for breaking the agreement. At twenty past two, Helen had still not arrived. She was obviously digging her heels in to the very end.

Eventually, I saw a yellow taxi coming up the road very slowly and it pulled up on the opposite side of the road to us. It was Helen and Vangelis and I could see Christopher waving to me in the back. Helen's face was a picture of complete and utter frustration. She was obviously very annoyed, but I didn't care. I was annoyed too that she had dared to be so late just to prove a childish immature point. Suzi was eager to run across the road to meet Christopher, but I stopped her. "They must come over to us," I said firmly.

"It's my turn to lay down the rules. I'm determined to rub their noses in it."

It was a long ten minutes before Helen brought Christopher over to us and when she did; her face was full of bitterness. I loved that moment as I knew Helen wasn't happy that Suzi was here with me. Helen was very jealous and didn't like the idea of her being near Christopher. She started to ramble on - I must do this and that and I must ring her every day. I just nodded my head and smiled. All I wanted to do was to get away with my son so I could cherish the time we had together. I didn't even say goodbye to Helen. I just picked up Christopher's small suitcase and walked away holding his hand.

We stayed on Aegina, the same Greek Island as we did before. We knew the place very well and we had plenty of friends there. We knew Christopher would love the island as there was a lovely beach where he could go swimming and there were plenty of other things of interest he would like. We stayed in the Oasis Hotel for two weeks. It was ideal for us as it had its own swimming pool and wasn't far from the beach, shops and bars.

The first few days were spent getting to know Christopher again and for him to get to know Suzi. Even though he seemed very happy to be with me, we did notice a few abnormal things he was doing. He wouldn't sleep inside the bed because he had been told the hotel might be dirty. He had also been instructed not to swim in the swimming pool as it would be full of people's germs and when we sat at the table, we had to clean it before we ate anything.

On one occasion, he had an accident in his pants and he started to cry. I had to calm him down and told him he was not to worry. On another occasion, he had a blister on his foot. He was very upset and begged me not to tell his mother.

I considered he must have been psychologically damaged with the kind of environment he lived in at Maria's house. I had seen that with my own eyes during my early visits to Greece. Maria always seemed crazy and Christopher wasn't allowed to play inside the house in case he broke anything. She was smothering him, preventing him from doing all the normal things boys do as they are growing up. He wasn't allowed to play out on his own or have sleepovers with his friends. He was even taken to and picked up from school in case I might be there to snatch him back. I tried to put all this out of my mind and for the time I had with him, I wanted to give him all the love he craved.

Christopher was getting pretty close to Suzi. He held her hand a lot and I allowed her take him out a few times so they could spend some time together and get to know each other.

Christopher picked some red flowers for her from a plant outside a white stone house near our hotel. He was bonding with Suzi which made me very happy. Suzi would never replace Helen, she knew that, but she was beginning to care for him and that was good. She took him on the beach to go swimming with him. As the holiday progressed, we became a family.

I phoned Helen while we were there and told her in no uncertain terms that I wasn't happy about the way Christopher was being brought up. "He's frightened of getting dirty, for God's sake, in case he'll be punished. You don't punish a child for getting a bit grubby! While Christopher is with me, he will do all the normal things children do," I told her, not hiding the venom in my voice. "It's all part and parcel of growing up. I am taking him swimming in the sea and in the pool and if he wants to get dirty playing, so be it." I didn't wait for her response. I put the phone down before she had the chance to object.

It felt brilliant being a father again and having a say in Christopher's upbringing. I was so happy being involved in his life. I had missed kissing him goodnight and holding him. I had missed all the simple things being a dad brings. I intended to cherish all the times I spent with him. As the days went by, I could see a change for the better in Christopher. He was so loving, full of fun and joy. I introduced him to Mike, my Greek friend whose dad owned Mike's Bar. Christopher spent a lot of time with Mike and went on the back of his moped around Agia Marina. They became very close. Another thing I noticed with Christopher was he wouldn't speak English to people as he was embarrassed. He always spoke Greek even if they could only speak English. It was clear that Maria was trying to destroy his English culture and wipe his memories of England from his mind.

I tried my best with Christopher during the days we were together. I told him that he must be proud of where he was born. He was an English boy with an English father and he had English relatives. I told him that he must love his mother and his father. I would never try to turn him against Helen as I suspected, she was doing as far as I was concerned. Hopefully, he would understand as he grew older.

We spent some fantastic times during my first access with him. We went swimming every day and we went fishing too most days. We also went on a boat trip to Poros and we did all the normal things a normal family would do together. All too quickly, the days passed by and as it came close to the time for going home, Christopher's mood changed. I could see he was very upset. On the last night, we went to Mike's Bar where he previously had been having a laugh with Mike and playing pool with him. That night Christopher wasn't interested. He wanted to be near me. He wouldn't leave my side and he held onto my hand all night. He held me so tight and he didn't want to let go. He drew his mouth close to my ear and whispered, "I love you, Daddy. I love you very much. You will come and see me again, won't you?"

Tears came into my eyes. I felt so sad in my heart for this little boy, my son, Christopher whom I loved more than life itself. I knew I would see him and I knew I would be back to Greece, but I must convince Christopher of that. "I love you, Chris. Always remember that. I shall be here for you forever."

We strolled down to the harbour where all the fishing boats were moored. Christopher held my hand and Suzi's hand and we sat down and gazed across the sea with sadness in our hearts. With Christopher in my arms, I allowed the tears to flow. Soon I would have to take him home to Piraeus where I knew Helen and her family would be waiting for him. Christopher was very tired. The emotional stress had taken its toll. I carried him to the hotel, undressed him and put him in to bed.

I stayed awake all night just looking at him as I stroked his arm, his hair and his hand. I wished that one day he would be free to be a normal child who wouldn't suffer being away from his father. I couldn't help hoping his Greek family would be punished one day for the hurt they have caused me and my beautiful little boy, Christopher. He had suffered being caught in the middle of two families who were at war with each other. Those thoughts broke my heart.

The morning dawned and I was still awake with all my thoughts. I saw the sunrise, but it was time to wake Christopher. I had to be strong and not show any emotion. I didn't want to upset Christopher. We had our breakfast and the atmosphere was muted. I could see Suzi was upset and I knew she had grown very much attached to Christopher during that holiday. Our suitcases were already packed and when it was time to go, I held Christopher close and told him not to be sad. I would be back to see him soon. He cheered up a little and on our way back on the boat, he held onto me so tight, it was a miracle I didn't cry again. We sat on the top deck looking across the sea and it wasn't long before he saw the shores of Athens. As we drew closer, he told me he loved me and made me promise that I would come again soon.

When we landed in Piraeus, it hit home that my first time with Christopher was coming to an end. Helen and Vangelis took Christopher without any communication between us as they climbed into Vangelis' taxi. Christopher waved goodbye and I fell in to Suzi's arms and wept. The taxi had gone out of sight now and he was gone.

The flight home seemed longer than usual. I had spent a short time with my son and I was supposed to be happy, but I still felt a sad loss. I shut my eyes and tried to be positive telling myself I would be seeing him again, but it didn't stop the tears. I just wanted to hold him in my arms forever.

For the next few years, I carried on seeing Christopher and travelled to Greece as often as possible. I stayed with him in Athens for Easter and the summer and went whenever I could, to visit him. I was determined to be part of his life and I was not letting that go. I had fought too hard to get this far and I would not let it all end now.

Chapter 22 – Amy Louise.

I married Suzi in October 2000. Our relationship had grown through those dark days of sadness and heart-break in Greece. She had stood by my side through thick and thin including the Greek courts. She had shared my tears on our special journeys to Greece. When we found out that Suzi was pregnant, it meant my life had gone full circle. I telephoned Christopher when the scan showed I was going to have daughter. During later telephone calls, he had been so upset because Maria and Helen had told him I wouldn't want him now.

I was furious. What sort of people would do a thing like that? I reassured him hundreds of times that my love for him would never die and I would always be there for him. I talked to him about his little sister all the way through Suzi's pregnancy. I want him to be a part of it and know that we would be a family together. I would carry on seeing him whenever I could, to make sure he knew I was there, to give him my love.

When I had found out Suzi was pregnant, I finally plucked up the courage to go into Christopher's room for the first time since he was abducted in 1998. In 2002, it was three years since he had been taken out of my life. I open the door slowly and it felt like we had never been apart. I looked around to take everything in. I could see his little school uniform where Helen had left it on his bed. His toys and school desk were still there. Why I had to remind myself of that, I don't know. I hadn't removed them so they had to be there. The moment was overwhelming. I looked in his drawers and his clothes were there. Around his bed were his teddy bears. I lay on his bed and I could smell him and see his presence all around me. I cried a million tears and fell asleep.

Suzi woke me. "You've been asleep for four hours. Are you all right?"

I looked down and I had one of Christopher's teddies in my arms. "I'll be okay," I told her. "Coming in here has made me feel the pain of the abduction all over again. I'll have to pack all this stuff away. It's the only way to ease my mind." I packed all his clothes and teddy bears into bags so I could show him one day if he ever came to England. It would confirm how much I loved him and how much I treasured everything about him.

I put the bags in the attic and set about stripping the walls and redecorating the room as a nursery for Amy Louise. The whole scenario was painful, but I had to keep telling myself that my daughter was not replacing him.

Suzi came in the room and held me in her. "This is a new chapter in your life, Ian," she said quietly. "Christopher has a sister. All the wallpaper and the curtains and his furniture are immaterial. He knows you will always love him and one day he will have his own room again."

I visited him in Athens and took him to Aegina to make sure he wasn't left out throughout Suzi's nine months of pregnancy. In July 2002, I visited him again just before the birth of my daughter. Because of the imminent birth, Suzi didn't go with me. It was only a three day visit and we stayed in Omonia Square away from prying eyes. I showered him with so much love and affection. I just wanted to reassure him that I would return soon with his little sister.

We had already picked the name Amy and I asked Christopher to choose a second name. "Louise," he said excitedly. "I like the name Louise and Amy Louise sounds nice." From that very moment, I hoped that Christopher and Amy Louise would have a special bond. When I received a phone call from Suzi to say she was in hospital, I had to cut my holiday short and book an early flight back. Telling Christopher I had to go home to England a day early was very difficult for me, but I told him that one day he would understand. I took him home to Helen's house and we walked up that wretched hill of tears that had featured so prominently in my life. I kissed Christopher goodbye and told him I would see him soon with his little sister, Amy Louise.

I arrived in England in time to see the birth of my beautiful daughter. I held her in my arms and she looked so much like Christopher had looked when he was born. I kissed her cheek. Holding Amy Louise for the first time created that special bond between father and daughter. My children would always be very special to me. I had tears of joy running down my cheeks, but my thoughts went back to Greece and my son, Christopher. I wanted so much to tell him he had he a beautiful sister.

The press wanted to publicise the birth of Amy Louise and they went to the hospital with a photographer to take pictures of us. The photographer was Nigel Taggart who was arrested in Greece in 1999 with Matthew Taylor. I had big smile on my face as I shook his hand and told him that at last something good had come out of that sad Greek tragedy.

Chapter 23 – Brother and sister

In December 2002, we travelled to Greece. It was a completely new experience in that I was accompanied by my wife Suzi and my new daughter, Amy Louise. I was very excited and could hardly wait to arrive in Athens. I held Amy Louise on my lap as she was only just over four months old. I looked into her beautiful blue eyes and I could see Christopher. She was so like he was when he was a baby. Her cute little smile meant everything to me. She was such a good baby and she slept in my arms until we landed in Greece.

Athens airport was very familiar to me and I felt relaxed that Helen and Vangelis would not be waiting outside to meet me. All the bad stuff was becoming a distant memory and my life was much happier. This trip to Greece had to be a most memorable one for two reasons. It would be my first Christmas with Christopher since he was abducted in 1998 and he would meet his baby sister for the first time. Because we would only have five days together, I wanted to cherish every second I spent with Christopher and remember them forever.

We had arranged to meet Helen in Piraeus at six o'clock outside the Metro station. We made our way there by train. I was bubbling with excitement and I was wondering what kind of reaction Christopher would have towards his little sister. When we arrived, I could see Helen and Christopher waiting on the platform. Helen deliberately avoided looking at Amy Louise. I would have thought curiosity would have got the better of her, but she showed no interest in the baby at all. I knew deep down that she was unhappy and jealous because I had moved on in my life.

I was holding Amy Louise in my arms and I bent down to Christopher and said, "This is your little sister." I watched his nervous little smile and put Amy Louise's hand on his face. "Look, you are nearly the same. You have the same blood."

I was fairly sure that Helen would have grilled Christopher before they came out and told him not to pay too much attention to Amy Louise. My views were confirmed later that day when Christopher suddenly announced, "Amy Louise isn't my proper sister, is she? Mummy told me."

Ian & Suzi in Greece with Christopher and baby Amy Louise

I had to laugh. Helen was growing more like her mother, Maria. Every day she lived with her, would make her the clone of her mother and that did not bode well for anybody. Back in the hotel, Christopher sat next to Amy Louise. He was playing with her. It warmed my heart to see that we had a complete family now. As we unpacked our cases, Christopher gave me a small present for Amy Louise. It was a baby rattle and he was so thrilled to give it to her.

"Why don't you sit on the bed and play with your little sister," I suggested. "You can get to know each other."

"Okay," he replied timidly.

Suzi and I watched as Christopher moved slowly nearer to Amy Louise. He was quite nervous with her and he just stared at her for a little while. "Why don't you let her sit on your knee," Suzi said to him. "Come on. Sit in that chair and I'll put her on your lap."

He was fascinated by her. After a short time, he was playing with her and kept shouting, "Daddy, Amy Louise is smiling at me!"

"That's because she loves you," I told him and he smiled lovingly at the baby on his lap.

On Christmas morning, he opened all of his present from Suzi and me. We had bought him a guitar that we knew he wanted, a Bolton Wanderers strip and various other things.

It was a very special occasion for me. It was our first Christmas together since 1998 and it felt wonderful. My thoughts momentarily drifted back to the first Christmas after the abduction. I had bought some presents for Chris and put them under the Christmas tree. I had done that for the first few years we were apart hoping that he would come back home.

We had our Christmas dinner in the hotel and it was a very happy occasion. We all wore Christmas hats and I had taken Christmas crackers, tinsel and a miniature Christmas tree. We had a fantastic day celebrating it like a British traditional Christmas. Finally, we ended the day singing Christmas carols. It was a day I shall never forget.

For the next few days we went round all the tourist areas of Plaka and to the famous Acropolis. Personally, I never tired of seeing that beautiful monument and historical treasure.

Christopher pushed Amy Louise's pram and each day they were growing closer in their brother/sister relationship. I watched them playing together every day and every night and couldn't prevent tears from trickling down my cheeks. Each night Christopher kissed Amy Louise goodnight and stroked her face. It was a lovely, touching scene and I treasure the memories of his bonding with his little sister.

All too soon, the final day arrived. Christopher was very quiet, because he knew I had to leave him behind. On the train to Piraeus, he held Amy Louise in his arms. It was sad moment for him, but a very special moment. I felt happy in the thought they had now bonded and I couldn't ask for more than that. On the bus to Perama, there was sadness in Christopher's eyes. He pushed Amy Louise up the hill of tears, all the away to Helen's house. It was a slow walk up to the house in the dark, but I have to say the house looked incongruously welcoming as it was well lit.

We left Christopher at the entrance and said our goodbyes. Christopher was crying. He didn't want us to leave him, but I told him I would be back soon. I hated leaving him like that, but I had no choice. He kissed Amy Louise and told her he loved her. We watched him walking up the stairs and I could hear Maria saying to him, "Go and have a showers then straight to bed."

As we were walking away from the house I said to Suzi, "Same old crazy Maria. Things never change." I wished I had heard her saying she missed him, but I didn't. How sad.

Chapter 24 – Continued access in Greece only.

I tried to see Christopher whenever I was able. Sometimes I went on my own and sometimes Suzi and his little sister, Amy Louise went with me. On one particular trip in July 2003, we travelled to Athens with Amy Louise who was nearly a year old. She was saying quite a few words and we had taught her to say Christopher. She wasn't quite walking, but she was a bit more grown up than the last time Christopher had seen her. She was full of smiles, had beautiful blonde hair and the most beautiful blue eyes.

We were staying on the island of Aegina again, a place that held a special place in my heart. We had already arranged with Helen to meet us at the port in Piraeus. As usual she arrived. It seemed she had no sense of time and was determined to mess up our plans. Arriving an hour after the arranged time, was so typical of her.

I had Amy Louise in my arms when a yellow taxi pulled up. I knew it was Vangelis and I totally blanked out his stare. Helen got out with Christopher and she looked at me with no emotion whatsoever. That didn't bother me in the slightest, especially when Christopher ran over to me and called out excitedly, "Daddy!"

I handed over Amy Louise to Suzi and then I picked up Christopher and held him in my arms. "I told you I'd be back with your little sister," I said loudly so that Helen could hear. "She has missed you."

We travelled by boat to Aegina and Christopher held Amy Louise on his lap. When she said, "Christopher," his face lit up and he laughed and joked with her all the way to Aegina.

He tried to communicate with Amy Louis more and more and he loved it when Amy Louise smiled and laughed with him. When we arrived at Agia Marina, he took over the pram pushing duties and wouldn't let us anywhere near it. Suzi and I smiled at each other. "Looks like we are redundant," she said.

After we settled in the hotel, we went to Mike's bar. Mike was a good friend to us and his bar was always our first port of call. When we introduced Amy Louise, Mike said straight away that she looked like Christopher. Chris was delighted. "She has to look like me, because she's my sister," he said proudly. Later, we went for a walk along the beach and Christopher insisted that we stopped for a while and he made some sandcastles for Amy Louise.

Suzi and I sat back during the holiday and allowed Christopher to have Amy Louise to himself within reason. We loved the way he was growing close to her and we wanted to encourage it. We went to the sea one day and Christopher was in his element. He put Amy Louise in a little plastic dinghy and pushed her along in the water. Amy Louise enjoyed it so much. She kicked her little feet in the water and laughed with her little baby giggles much to everyone's delight.

Christopher was devoted to his sister. On the way back to the hotel, he went in to a shop and bought Amy Louise a little flower. It was a white rose and he kissed her on the cheeked as he gave it to her. "I love you," he whispered and it brought a tear to my eye.

It reminded me of when I gave his mother a red rose in Corfu when I first met her. Like father like son I thought. Amy Louise was very beautiful and so was Christopher's mother, but that's all in the past now.

We strolled back to hotel with Christopher pushing the pram as usual. We cleaned up and dressed ready for dinner. Christopher was playing with Amy Louise on the bed when she fell off and banged her head. Christopher was shocked. He jumped off the bed and held her in arms, rocking her until she stopped crying. When she calmed down, I checked Amy Louise was alright and she was soon laughing and giggling again.

At meal times, Amy Louise was having baby food and yogurts which Christopher fed her. They were so close, almost inseparable. Suzi and I took a back seat while Christopher was around. It was important for them both to spend as much time together as possible.

In the evening we stayed in the hotel bar and met a couple from Leeds, Jean and John. They became very attached to

Christopher and Amy Louise and we told them the truth about Christopher's situation. We became very friendly with them and went around with them for the rest of the holiday. They were really good company and very entertaining. They were both in their sixties, always smiling and telling us funny stories. Jean was very comical and she made me laugh many times. Each night in the bar, she sprayed her arms and legs with mosquito spray, but she still got bitten. I used to giggle when she put scented candles on the table and lit them up to keep the mosquitoes away. It never worked. I called her Buffy the vampire as she had so many candles on her table. It was hilarious. Every time we met up with her, she had more bites. It looked like she had chicken pox.

John and Jean were like family to us. In such a short time, we became very close to them. They gave Amy Louise and Christopher so much love and they bought them everything from clothes to toys. We went on a boat trip to Poros together and walked round the shops and the cobbled streets. Later we went for a meal in a small cafe in a side street. It wasn't very big, but looked very clean and the waiters were very friendly and polite. Afterwards, we walked along the beach and occasionally stopped for a coffee, or soft drinks. We stayed for a few hours then we made our way back to Aegina.

John and Jean were leaving the following morning so we decided to have a late night with them. We decided to let Amy Louise sleep in her pram. The evening was unusually quiet because we were sad that John and Jean were leaving us. Christopher was playing with Amy Louise on the floor as she had learned to crawl and at times she tried to walk. I noticed that John was becoming upset as the evening wore on and Buffy? Well, she just carried on complaining about her mosquito bites!

We made our way back to the hotel and arranged to meet up in the morning to wave them off on the ferry boat. We kissed them both good night. John picked up Amy Louise kissed her cheek and then he picked up Christopher up and hugged him tightly. Not being able to hide his emotions, he walked off. Jean hugged both children and went to their room.

Suzi and I stood and watched them go into their room. I had a lump in my throat as I had really grown fond them. The following morning we had a breakfast together in a cafe on the marina. I couldn't be bothered to eat much and Suzi was the same. When the time came to wave them off, we met them at the marina where the ferry boat was to leave. We hugged each other warmly. John had tears in his eyes when we kissed Amy Louise and Christopher; he was clearly upset. He picked up the suitcases and walked onto the ferry boat. He was very sad to leave us. Jean or Buffy as I called her, realised he was upset. She kissed Christopher and Amy Louise and followed John onto the boat.

We watched the boat leave across the deep blue sea as John and Jean waved goodbye until till they was out of sight. We kept in touch for a long time after that holiday. John and Jean became Amy Louise's God-parents and later they made a special trip to Bolton for her confirmation.

On our final day, we went swimming and visited the shops. That evening, we spent in Mike's bar. We were all very quiet. When holidays come to an end, it's difficult not to get too emotional. I knew Christopher was upset because he wasn't as chirpy as usual with Amy Louise. He just held her hand and stared into her eyes. We didn't stay long in Mike's bar. We went for a final stroll on the beach and sat on the same rock I had sat on many times before on my final nights on Aegina. We looked at the deep blue sea and watched the waves washing over the rocks. Suzi put her arm round me and whispered in my ear. "Don't cry, Ian. Christopher is already very upset because we have to leave him behind."

I looked at Christopher with Amy Louise asleep in the pram next to him. He was stroking her hair and her hand. I simply had to go for a walk. I couldn't stand to see him so upset like that. It was such an emotional time for him. I walked a short way along the beach, wiping away my tears. I had had so many upsets in Greece. I had said so many goodbyes there and each time it was getting harder and harder. I wondered how many more times I would be able to do it.

When I returned to the rock, they had gone. Suzi had taken them back to the hotel. I must have been gone for over an hour without realising it. I sat down on the rock rested my head on my arms. Once more, I broke down crying. All my emotions came flooding out. Much as I didn't want to remember all the troubles and all times I had had with Helen, the court cases and when I received the phone call that fateful day when Helen told me she wasn't coming home, my mind was swamped with them. How many more of these visits could I endure? Greece was turning into a nightmare and it was destroying me. I went to back to the hotel room. Christopher was asleep in Amy Louise's bed. Suzi was fast asleep too and I was exhausted both physically and mentally.

When I woke up the following morning, Christopher was already awake and so was Amy Louise. They were playing together. We had our last breakfast together and walked to the ferry boat. Strangely, Christopher didn't push Amy Louise's pram. He wanted to hold on to my hand. We made our way onto the ferry and the journey back was long and tearful. Christopher was crying and I held him in my arms all the way back.

When we landed in Piraeus, Helen was there with Vangelis in his yellow taxi. We didn't have much time to say our proper goodbyes. Christopher held Amy Louise and kissed her cheek for the final time. He had no idea when he would see her again. I held Christopher for a few moments and then I kissed him goodbye. He kissed Suzi. Leaning over Amy Louise's pram, he whispered, "Goodbye my little sister. I love you." He looked at me with tears rolling down his face and walked away. As the taxi pulled away, he waved and then he was gone. Suzi held me in her arms and we made our way to the coach that would take us to the airport in Athens.

I carried on visiting Christopher for a number of years and each year he was growing older and more mature and each year it became harder and harder to say goodbye.

Chapter 25 – Goodbye Christopher.

After years of fighting in Greece, I had one more court case to face. I had to fight for Christopher to visit England. I had already fought so hard to take Christopher home to the land of his birth. The number of years I had been visiting him in Greece and saying goodbye to him had taken its toll on me both physically and mentally. I was worn out; a mere shell of my former self. I had come to a decision to let him go as he too was suffering seeing me leaving him. Not only that, his family in Greece put pressure on him every time I visited him and with the court case coming up, it would get worse for him. If I went ahead with it and failed, I had to let go so he could be freed of any troubles in his life and interference from his mother and more so from Maria and Vangelis.

The trip to Greece in 2007 would live with me forever. I had been visiting Christopher since the year 2000 when I was granted access to see him. From the age of nine he had been allowed to see me only in Greece. We had spent some very special times together, in Athens and on the island of Aegina. Now Christopher was fifteen years old and had matured into a handsome young man. He understood a lot more things about what happened between his mother, Helen and me. Over the years, he had sussed out all the tricks Maria had got up to by trying to stop me seeing him.

I waited for Christopher at the port of Piraeus as usual. Vangelis dropped him off and then left. We travelled by boat to Aegina and had fun as usual on the way. Christopher had no idea what I was going to say to him, but I intended to wait a few days before I informed him of my decision. We arrived at the hotel unpacked and went out for a meal. In the evening, he wanted to go to Mike's bar. We chatted about Amy Louise and Adam his brother who had been born in 2005. Christopher had never seen Adam, only in photographs I had sent to him in Greece. Demands of family life and family expenses prevented us all going together, so I had visited a couple of time a year since 2003.

We went swimming as usual as he was now a very good swimmer, unlike his dad. Chris was growing up and was a typical teenager, looking at girls and admiring them like all young boys do. He occasionally went out on his own for a while enjoying the freedom he didn't have with his mother. I left him to his own devices realising that young boys need to live a little. We were there for only a week and it was on our third day, I decided to tell him what I was going to do.

I didn't allow Christopher to drink alcoholic drinks, but he had small ouzo now and again. I considered that to have a small drink while under my supervision would do no harm. It was part of growing up. While we were in Mike's bar I tried to explain. "I'm not putting any more pressure on you coming to England," I said. "I'm going to cancel the appeal for access in England."

Christopher just looked at me and said nothing. I had to speak from the heart and hope he would understand.

"I'm sorry for all the troubles between your mother and me. I tried so hard to take you home. I can't tell you how much I suffered. I didn't go into your room for nearly three years because I was too frightened to go in."

"What were you frightened of, Dad?" Chris asked.

"I was haunted by the memories of you and I thought that if I went into your room, I would become very depressed. When I met your mother, I fell deeply in love with her, but I had to smuggle her out of Greece because Maria and Vangelis wouldn't allow her to fall in love and lead her own life." Christopher nodded and smiled almost as if he knew exactly what I was talking about. I told him about that fatal phone call when his mother informed me she wasn't going home with me and when Maria threw my suitcase down the stairs. "I think you need to know all these things and I hope you understand that I have to let you get on with your own life in Greece. You are Greek now and you are used to the Greek way of life. You speak Greek and your life is here. I have to accept that now that you have been here for nine years. As long as I fight in the Greek courts to take you home, you will get a lot pressure from your mother and her family, because they don't want me to be a part of your life."

I needed him to understand it wasn't about me anymore. "You are old enough to understand and in time, you'll be old enough to decide what you want."

Christopher just sat quietly and listened.

"I will always love you as will your sister and brother and your family in England. You have to believe that. All I ask is that you enjoy your life and if you ever need me, you know where I am."

I hugged and kissed him and we both cried, but I asked him not forget me. I'm your dad and I will always love you."

I knew Christopher was sad, but he realised I was giving him the freedom to live his life without pressure from Helen and her family. Cancelling the appeal would make life easier for him.

We spent the last few days having fun and generally having a good time. On our last day we sat on the same rock we had sat on before with his little sister, Amy Louise on our last visit as a family. Chris rested his head on my shoulder and we looked out to sea and listened to the waves splashing against the rocks. "Do you remember when we looked out to sea and I told you England was out there. I hope that one day we will be there together," I told him gently.

I don't know what Christopher was thinking, maybe I ought to have asked, but he must have realised that we wouldn't see Aegina again as a family and that our lives would be different from then on. I can only guess what he was thinking. I knew he loved me very much. I simply didn't want to see him suffer anymore and I hoped that one day he would realise why I let him go. I certainly know I did it because I loved him.

We said our goodbyes when we landed in Piraeus. We hugged each other, said we loved each other and he walked away out of my life. I headed for the airport. The flight home was sad, but I consoled myself that I had so many wonderful memories.

For the next few years, my life in England changed for the better. I had no worries about Christopher. The pressure seemed to have been lifted off my shoulders. I started to smile more, but I never forgot Christopher. He was always in my heart. When my son, Adam was born, Christopher couldn't see him. I knew he loved his sister, Amy Louise, but with my new wife Suzi and two children in England, my family was complete. Christopher wasn't there, but he would always be a part of me and of my family. I had to move on with my life.

Christopher and I lost contact we lost all contact and although I left him with a broken heart, I did it all for the love of Christopher.

Chapter 26 – Making contact again.

Three years passed since the last time I had seen or heard from him. Something from deep inside told it was perhaps time to go and see him again. We would be both stronger and able to cope with all the pressures of the separation. Christopher was nineteen, a young man who was old enough to make his own decisions without any interference from Helen or Maria.

In June 2010, I flew out to Athens without telling Chris I was going. I thought I would surprise him and as I was only going there for four days, I wanted to make the most of it. I stayed in Omonia Square again and after I unpacked I went out. I rang Christopher from a cafe and Maria answered the phone. "Is Christopher there?" I asked.

She went very quiet and then shouted to Christopher. "Your dad is on the phone."

I imagined Christopher rushing to the phone. "Hi Dad, how are you?"

"I am good, Chris. How are you?" I answered.

"I'm fine, thanks," he said. "Where are you?"

"I'm in cafe in Omonia Square," I told him.

He went very quiet. I don't think he believed me or he was in total shock. I would have loved to have seen his face. It must have been a picture. It brought back fleeting memories of when I ran away from home to Paris when I was fourteen years old. I was held in the British Embassy in Paris while one of the Embassy officials rang my mother and told her, "We have your son here."

"Where is he?" she had asked.

When the Embassy official replied, "He is in the British embassy in Paris," my mother must have collapsed with shock the way I was imagining Christopher now after three years of no contact.

"Do you want to meet me?"I asked.

"Of course I do, yes," he replied as though it were a foregone conclusion.

We met outside the Metro in Piraeus, the same place I used to meet Helen all those years before. He was not shy or nervous when he saw me. He just hugged me and asked me how I had been.

I told him I had missed him more than he would ever know and he said he'd missed me too. It had been twelve years since he had been abducted in 1998 when he was seven years old and it felt like a life-time ago.

I looked at Christopher. He was older and a lot more mature; a lad without any fears. I was quite taken aback. He talked with a lot confidence and although his English was fine, he spoke with a Greek accent.

I decided to speak openly and honestly. "I want you to come to England to see your home where you were born and to see your family, Amy Louise and Adam, the brother you have never seen and Grandma and Granddad. They have missed you too all these years."

He smiled and said, "I will; I'd love to."

We both smiled happily and I held his hand as I said, "I will have to let you know when is best, but what about your mother and Maria? Are you sure they won't try to stop you."

He burst out laughing and said, "Dad, I'm nearly nineteen, for God's sake. It's my life."

I had waited so long to hear him to say that - fourteen years in fact. I just couldn't believe it. We chatted for few hours and the beer was flowing. When he was going home, he told me he loved me.

"I love you too. Always did, always will," I told him. "I'll meet you at your mother's tomorrow at three o'clock." After that, I happily made my way back to the hotel. Once there, I opened my suitcase to reveal all the love letters Helen and I had written, along with the red rose I had given her in 1990. I was on a mission to put Helen out of my head forever. I rang Helen the following morning and asked her if I could see her.

She told me to be there about three o'clock in the afternoon. I arrived on time and she was waiting for me. She invited me in and made coffee for me. As I was drinking it, I gave her the love letters and the red rose. She sat down and began to cry. "I am so sorry for the things I did," she said. "Can you ever forgive me?"

I thought carefully about what I should say before I spoke. "It's a long time ago now. Christopher is older and I have moved on in my life. I will always care for you, because you were my first true love and the mother of my child."

She wept again and for a split second, I wanted to comfort her, but I stopped myself. I silently reminded myself that this was the girl whom I married, who stole my child and took him from me and his country. The suffering and heartbreak and all the court battles destroyed any love I ever had for her. She had no life in Greece; no money, no job and I believed her relationship with Maria wasn't good. I stayed with her for a couple of hours until Christopher came in and asked, "Are you ready, Dad?"

"I am," I told him and then I turned to Helen. "Goodbye, Helen," I walked away and out of her life forever.

Christopher and I spent the final days of my stay together, having long talks into the night and on the last night; I shook his hand and told him again that I loved him. "See you soon." He walked away into the night and the following morning I flew home, full of hope.

Chapter 27 – Homecoming at last.

After the visit to Greece to renew my contact with Christopher, I arrived back in England full of hope and expectations. He was going to come home for the first time since 1998. It had seemed a lifetime to me and now all the court battles and the journeys of tears; all the suffering and the heartache was coming to an end. My son was finally coming home to see me and his family.

I had arrived by taxi at my new home in Smedley Avenue in Great Lever. Moving out of Alder Street which held so memories of Christopher and Helen finally made me leave that part of my past behind. Buying the house in Smedley Avenue was a definite plus in my life. With Christopher coming home, it would show him that we all had a new life, a life of which he could be a part. Amy Louise was so happy and excited that her brother was coming home, but Adam was quite nervous as he had never seen his brother so he didn't know what to expect. Having a big brother was alien to him.

My mother was philosophical when I telephoned to tell her Christopher was coming home. "I hope he arrives," she said. "Let's wait and see if he gets on the plane."

"He's nineteen now, Mum," I told her. "He's not the little boy you last saw. He's his own person and he's matured into a good looking young man - just like his dad!"

I booked the flight for April and it was only a matter of weeks before he would arrive. He would be staying for two weeks and I intended to make his visit wonderful for us all. Those few weeks before, seemed like a lifetime. All I thought about, day and night was Christopher is coming home.

I tried to concentrate at work, but it was very difficult. I made sure I was fully occupied and went for frequent walks around the Jumbles Country Park in Bolton. Most weekends I watched my beloved Bolton Wanderers on Saturdays with Amy Louise and Adam who are avid fans like me. We began the countdown to Christopher's arrival a few days before. We had been speaking to each other on Skype and he had told me he was excited and looking forward to seeing his sister, Amy Louise and his brother, Adam.

The night before he was due to arrive I went out with my good friend, Mark Slater who I had known for a number of years. He had always been good company when I needed it and we used to go to Bolton Wanderers matches together. I didn't sleep much that night. Amy Louise jumped into our bed and squeezed in between Suzi and me. She had the same problem I had; she was too excited to sleep.

The following morning, Amy Louise went to school with Adam. She was very annoyed because she didn't want to go, but I had arranged a surprise for her and asked that I might take her out of school at lunchtime. I had made an excuse that she had a hospital appointment and felt justified in using a little white lie on such a momentous occasion for our family. I went to pick her up and the teacher brought her out of class. She was so thrilled to see me. "Thanks, Dad!" she said excitedly.

Amy Louise and I went to the airport during the afternoon. She was eleven years old and hadn't seen Christopher since she was a one year old baby in Aegina, the island where I had made so many memories with Christopher. He wasn't due to land until five o'clock, but had given ourselves a couple hours to prepare for his arrival. I wanted to cherish the moment and had we been on the last minute, it would have spoiled the whole event. Amy Louise and I went for a coffee to pass the time. She was so excited, but she was also very nervous. I joked and laughed with her to try to calm her down, but she just became more and more nervous as the time came nearer to Christopher's arrival. She kept saying to me, "Will Christopher still remember me? Does he still love me?"

"He loves you very much so just calm down and cherish the moment," I told her with a smile on my face.

I couldn't hide my own excitement and certainly didn't want to. We finished our drinks and the plane had landed. We waited excitedly for him outside the exit where the travellers came through passenger control. Amy Louise held my hand and my emotions were mounting. My body was shaking with anticipation of his arrival.

Silly doubts were also creeping in to my head. What if Christopher had not got on plane?

What if Maria, the woman I hated so much and had so many battles with all those years ago, had stolen Christopher's passport?

All my fears turned to joy as Christopher came through the door and walked towards me smiling from ear to ear. It was difficult for me to believe he was finally home. All the sadness and trials and tribulations ebbed away when he said to me, "Hi, Dad." He hugged me and I felt him melt into my arms. "I love you, Dad."

He bent down to Amy Louise and hugged her. "Hi, little sister," he said.

I had to pinch myself to convince myself it wasn't a dream, but Christopher was home and back in my life. Even though it was only going to be for a short while, I knew I would cherish it forever.

We travelled back on the train and Amy Louise was all over Christopher. She was just gazing at him. I think it was more happiness than shock. I had spoken to Amy Louise about Christopher since the day she was born. I had told her everything that had happened in Greece, about Helen and Maria and the abduction, so we had created for her a special bond with Christopher. Every night before she went to sleep, she used to kiss Christopher's picture that was on the cabinet next to her bed. That was something really special.

When we arrived at the house, Suzi and Adam were waiting for us. Christopher knew Suzi very well from when we made the trips to Greece together. He hugged her and kissed Adam, the little brother he had never seen. We showed him his room and after a short while, I took him to our old house where he used to live in Alder Street, Great Lever. The next place I wanted him to see was his school, Saint William of York which wasn't far away, just a few minutes' walk. Christopher was going back in time to his childhood. I didn't speak to him as he seemed to be entranced as the memories came flooding back.

"What are you thinking, Chris?" I asked him as we approached the school.

"Everything," he said with a smile. "I can remember being here, but it seems a long time ago. I know I was happy here. This is very special to me."

After the brief visit into his past, we went back home. I sat back and watched him spend time with his English family, his memories re-surfacing and getting to know his little sister and brother. One of biggest moments was when I took him to his grandma's, the woman who had fought so hard for him in the Greek courts all that time ago. It was very emotional for my mother as she too had waited eleven years for this special day. She hugged him tightly and it was difficult for me to watch her eyes filling with tears, but to her credit, she pulled herself together and maintained her dignity. We spent the day chatting to Christopher, about his life and what he wanted to do in the future. We had so much to catch up on.

The press found out that Christopher was home and they came round to the house. I don't know how they found out, but I had told so many of my friends he was coming, so maybe one of them informed the Bolton Evening News. "Do you mind if these people ask you a few questions and take a few pictures?"

What will they want to know?" he asked.

"Just what you feel like coming home after so long," I told him.

"No problem," he said.

I had warned them not to talk about the abduction. I thought it was inappropriate at this point. However, they said they would to cover the surprise party I was arranging for Christopher, but I told them I would prefer them not to as it was a private occasion, just for him and his family.

Radio Bolton phoned me and asked if Christopher and I would do an interview about him coming home. They had found out from their contacts in the press. Again I asked Christopher beforehand and he agreed to do it. I was very surprised as I thought he might not want to talk publicly about personal stuff.

After all the interviews were over, I took Chris and his sister and brother to the Reebok Stadium to see my beloved Bolton Wanderers, the football team he supported when he was little boy. We all wore Bolton Wanderers tops and it was a very proud moment for me. Having my children following me as avid Bolton Wanderers supporters made me feel good.

On the way to the ground, lots of people came over and shook Christopher's hand. I don't think he realised how famous he had become with all the television and press coverage he had been given over the years.

After the match, I took him into the club shop and the manager gave him a pennant signed by all the Bolton Wanderers players for him to put on his wall in Greece. It was a proud and memorable day especially when our team won 2-0. Christopher thoroughly enjoyed it and that was all that mattered.

Phone calls came in fast and furious. Friends and family were all eager to ask about Christopher and when the news came out in the local paper that he was at home in England, he became a local celebrity. Wherever we went, people came over and hugged him.

The day came for his surprise party. We had put up balloons with the words 'Welcome Home' all over the front window and in the front room. I had made sure Christopher was out of the way spending some time with my sister, Pat who had agreed to bring him home around seven o'clock.

Friends and family started to come round, all waiting for Christopher with eager anticipation.

When he arrived, he opened the door and loud applause went up. It brought tears to my eyes. It was the special moment for which I had prayed all those years before. The night went well. Christopher was overcome. I don't think he had realised how much he had been missed by everybody. Time passed quickly. They say time flies when you're having fun and it was very true. It wasn't long before we had to say goodbye again. Amy Louise and I took him to the airport. We kissed and hugged and off he went. He turned round and waved and called out, "See you soon."

In May 2011, he kept his promise and came back home for two weeks, hoping to see Bolton Wanderers in the FA Cup final. Sadly, they had lost the semi final against Stoke City so it wasn't to be. Christopher visited again for another two weeks and the following year he came in December and spent his first Christmas in England since 1998. This time he was able to open the presents under the Christmas tree.

So this is my story, a journey which started in Corfu in 1990 where I met and fell in love with a Greek girl called Helen, my first true love. It was an incredible journey, full of tears and joy and heartbreak. Would I change any of it? Never in my wildest dreams.

My final message must go to Maria, the woman I grew to hate. Thank you for throwing my suitcase down the stairs, for saying my marriage was finished and that I would never see my son, Christopher again. Thank for giving me the strength to carry on.

All this was for the love of Christopher.

Epilogue.

After 56 years of years of my life, I can now look back and reflect on the good times and the bad times; the trials and tribulations I went through from being a small boy.

I was brought up in a three up, two down terraced house in Lee Street, in an old mill town in Lancashire called Farnworth. I was one of four brothers and three sisters; a close knit family brought up in impoverished times. Our clothes came from jumble sales; that was the norm in those days. Our staple diet was from the local chippy. We were sent there with a bowl to ask for chips, peas and scraps. Hoping to get a larger portion to feed our family made me feel like Oliver Twist, "Please sir can I have so have some more?"

I was often sent by my father, from whom I suffered years of bullying, to go and look for wood from the building sites. This was because we couldn't afford to buy coal to keep warm in the winter.

At our local school Saint Gregory's in Farnworth, my two brothers and I were used to being the subject of jokes on the school playground. We were called the Beatles because we all had the same hair styles. I'm sure my mum used to cut all our hair with a pudding basin on the head and short back and sides for the areas under the rim. "Thanks Mum!"

I lost count of the number times I ran away from home because of the bullying I received from the hands of my father. I will never forget the time when I was 14 years old and I ran away from home to Paris.

While I was there I was sleeping in the back of parked up wagons and stealing hot bread from the bakeries which they used to leave on trays in the early hours.

I was caught by the local police for my troubles.

I was then taken in style, in a police car, to the British Embassy in Paris. There an official telephoned my mother and told her that they had her son there.

She then replied, "Where is that?"

The embassy official then answered, "Paris."

I heard my mother reply "Paris! I'll bloody well kill him."

During my teenage years I was in and out trouble and I left home to make my own way in life.

I was in and out of relationships. I just couldn't settle with girls as we were always looking for different things.

The only real passion I had was following Bolton Wanderers home and away. This got me into all kinds of trouble all over the country.

Then one day I received a phone call from my mother to say my father was dying. I came home and made peace with him before he died, after all the years of hatred, I had felt towards him.

I stood at the funeral looking at his wreath. Suddenly I felt a loss which totally confused me. I stood there deep in thought. All I wanted in life was to be loved and I had a father who found it difficult to show or to tell me that.

I made a decision there and then that I had to turn my back on all my troubles and try to turn my life around. I had been drifting through life being rebellious and part of that was my father's fault. If he only he had given me love and attention maybe I could have done things differently in my life.

His passing coincided with a failed relationship and I decided to go on holiday after that and try to sort my life out. I stopped outside a travel agents and a holiday in Corfu was on offer. This was the start of a journey which would change my whole life forever.

I met and fell in love with a Greek girl called Helen and that first kiss would stay with me forever. I gave her a red rose which symbolised our love together which would result in a trip to Athens a few months later.

It was here I first met her mother Maria who would eventually be a thorn in my side and Vangelis, her step father who would later be involved in a web of deceit against me.

The beatings I received from her family only made me more determined to bring Helen to England.

In 1990 I made a secret return trip to Athens and met Helen on the hill near her house. I would later call it the hill of tears.

We settled in England and it wasn't long after that she presented me with a son who we named Christopher; a beautiful little boy who I adored and who would eventually be stolen on a family holiday in Athens in 1998 with my wife.

On that fatal day of 19th August I received a phone call of my wife Helen that she would not be returning to England.

This resulted in Maria throwing my suitcase down the stairs and me walking down the 'hill of tears' a broken man.

I will never forget that long flight home to England next to two empty seats which nearly resulted in me ending my life with an overdose of aspirin. My mother, who was my rock and inspiration, gave me the strength to carry on the fight in the Greek courts.

I then watched my mother who was destroyed in the witness box by Helen's lawyer for just standing by her son.

Not realising, Maria and Vangelis gave me more strength to carry on the fight to bring Christopher home.

I suffered and lost in the Greek courts but eventually won the right to see Christopher in Greece.

I stood by him till he was sixteen and it was then that I made a decision to let him go, to have a normal life and free of the pressures from my dispute with Helen's family.

Then after four years of losing contact with Christopher, I decided to return to Athens to ask him to come to visit me and his family England.

Christopher landed on English soil in April 2011, 12 years after being taken out of my life. He has now visited me three times up to 2014 when this story was published. We are in regular contact and I still hope that one day he will be with me in England, the country in which he was born.

Christopher, however, is settled in Greece. He has done his national service in the Greek army and matured into a fine, mature young man who will one day find his own way in life.

The last time I saw Helen was when I was on a mission to see Christopher in 2010, she was still single and unemployed. It was then that I decided to return to her the rose I had presented with love in Corfu in 1990. At the same time I gave her all the love letters she had sent to me all those years ago. I wanted closure. She asked me for my forgiveness and I agreed. Then I walked out of her life forever.

Maria and Vangelis are still together and no doubt Maria is still in control of their marriage and their finances which are now threatened by the Greek recession. As for me I have been married to Suzi since 1998 and have two beautiful children with her. They are Amy Louise who is now eleven and Adam who is now nine

My mother, my rock, is now 86 and still going strong but sadly she lost her husband Jack, my step-dad who I loved like a father. He died of cancer in April 2013.

So this is the end of all my journeys; a roller coaster ride, a Greek love affair that turned into a Greek tragedy and the fight of my life to be a father to Christopher.

If you asked me now would I ever change anything?

My answer would be only for the love of Christopher.

I rocked the cradle

I started a dream
I held you in my arms
I rocked your cradle
I kissed your cheek
I saw your lovely smile
I rocked you to sleep
Please don't cry
I stood and stared in to your sleeping eyes
And I saw me
I fell asleep
And one day you was gone
Forever a broken heart
An empty cradle
Pictures of you on the wall
Memories of you I will always keep
I kissed your cheek and now was gone
Empty spaces and empty room
Broken man with a broken dream
I kissed your cheek and you were gone
I finally died a broken man
Or was it just a dream

The path of tears
I went to Corfu and fell in love
With happiness and tears
A red rose, a symbol of our love
I watched her leave with sadness and tears
A kiss on the cheek and now she was gone
A journey to Athens with hope and in love
We walked the cobbled streets of the acropolis
Hand in hand full of love
The weeks passed by
A kiss on her cheek and she was gone
I couldn't live with memories
Living a part
I hitchhiked across to Greece
Full of love and hope
Love turned to tragedy
I was beaten and forced to say good bye
A kiss on the cheek and now she was gone
Journey home full off tears
A broken man with sadness
A broken heart which was dying
I flew to Greece undetected
I walked up the path of tears
I saw my only true love
My Helen
We escaped across different lands
We arrived in Lancashire a town of cobbled streets and
smoking chimneys
Bolton was our home
Where we soon bore a son
Christopher was born
On a fatal day a call of sadness

I kissed Christopher on his cheek and now he was gone
My suitcase thrown down the stairs
I walked down the path of tears a broken man
I finally died the whole world was crying
The joke was on me
The day I kissed his cheek and now he was gone
I knew our love would never die
I fought and lost in courts in a land far away
My thoughts went back to that sad day
I started to cry
My suitcase was thrown down the stares
I started to cry
They just looked at me
The joke was on me.
I walked down the path of tears a broken man
I kissed his cheek and now he was gone
I returned and fought in a land afar
I finally won
With tears of joy
We walked down the path of tears hand in hand
With tears full of joy
I kissed his cheek and now he was gone
He returned to me in my town
Bolton a town of cobbled streets and smoking chimneys
A town were the famous steeplejack was born
The joke was now on me
For the love of Christopher

Please don't ask me why you were taken. Part 1

Don't ask me why you and I would never die
When you were born I kissed your cheek and my bond for
you was born and you were mine
I knew my love for you would never die
I watched you grow
And Christmases would come and go
I knew when you were small my love for you would never
die
I held you so many times when you were small
Please don't cry
Don't ask me why but my love for you will never die
One day you were taken
Please don't ask me why
Don't ask me why you are so far away
Don't ask me why the times have passed us by
Someone else has moved in from so far away.
Now you are tall and all grown up
Please don't ask me why you were taken
Please don't cry
You and I and our will, will never die
My bond for you will always be true
My heart is broken
Please don't ask me why you were taken
Please don't cry
You and I will have that special love that will never die

I kissed your cheek when you were born and that will never
pass me by.

Please don't ask me why you were taken. Part 2

Please don't ask me why you were taken
I know you and I that our love would never die
I woke up one day and you were gone
Please don't ask me why you were so far away
My Christmases would come and go
Under the Christmas tree was so bare
Don't ask me why you were taken
Please don't cry
I walked down the path of tears all alone
A broken man please don't ask me why
A flight home with two empty seats
Don't ask me why the times just passed me by
I know you and I, our love will never die
Please don't ask me why you were taken
Please don't cry
Someone else has moved in from so far away .
Your room is empty
Toys of yours were aplenty
Please don't cry
All I have is your pictures on my empty walls
Don't ask me why but times have passed me by
I prayed so many times as my life was bare
Please don't cry
Your school was so close
I remember waving you goodbye
Please don't ask me why you were taken
I kissed your cheek for the final time that day when you were
taken
That bond I have for you will never die
I hope one day that bond will return
Because I know you and I, our love will never die

I looked in to the street where you used to play
Someone has moved in so far away
I kissed the cheek and I knew that my love would never die
and that you were mine
Please don't ask me why you were taken
I will never forget that day I kissed your cheek and you were
gone
Please don't ask me why you were taken
Please don't cry
I know you and I, our love will never die
I know that we are old but that cheek I kissed will ever be
mine

Please don't ask me why you were taken. Final part 3

Please don't ask me why you were taken
I fought so hard I won and I lost
Tears and joys were full of pain
Please don't cry
I stood and cried on the path of tears
The day I won
Tears were pride of joy
I reflected walking up that path of tears
I knew you and I, our love would never die
I held you in my arms
I said please don't cry
I kissed your cheek I knew you were mine
We walked down the path of tears with pride and joy
I pointed to a star and said one day you will be forever mine
We held each other and cried tears of joy
I knew you and I our love would never die
I waved my final good bye

I reflected on the journeys the oceans and lands afar
I fought so hard with tears and joy
I know one day that you will be forever mine
The path of tears will one day be a bad dream
Please don't cry
You came back in to my life
I knew that cheek I kissed that would be forever mine .
Times passed me by
A tragedy turned in to tears of pride and joy
Now I can forever smile

Forever you will be mine